Being
Eighty
Keyn Ahara

Joyful Awakening Books

Being Eighty

Keyn Ahara

What a Ride!
A book of inspiration and hope

Dr. Paula Bromberg

Being Eighty: Keyn Ahara
What a Ride!

For reproduction rights, contact
Dr. Paula Bromberg
E-mail: Goldoceandrive@gmail.com
Facebook:PaulaAmbikaBromberg

Publisher's Cataloging-in-Publication
Bromberg, Dr. Paula N.
Being Eighty: Keyn Ahara
What a Ride!
Dr. Paula N. Bromberg -- 1st Ed.
p. cm.
LCCN 2003112905
ISBN 978-0-9715474-4-5
1. Self-actualization. 2. Spiritual life.
3. Interpersonal relations. 4. New Age.
5. Personal growth. 6. Self-help.
I. Title.
BF637.S4B76 2004   158.1
                                   QBI03-700680

also available as an E-book

Printed in the United States of America

Photos: Dr. Paula Bromberg
Book design: The Book Couple/Dr. Paula Bromberg
Cover photograph: Dr. Paula Bromberg

Also by Dr. Paula Bromberg:

Notes from the Ocean, 2014

The Way of the Lover – A Way of Understanding

The Fifth Way – Life at its Best, 2020
    Hardcover—Limited Edition

Tantra, East West, Past/Present: Living Presence, 1995

Endeavor: A Journal in the Sufi Tradition, 1993

Sacred Psychology: The Path of the Heart, 1989

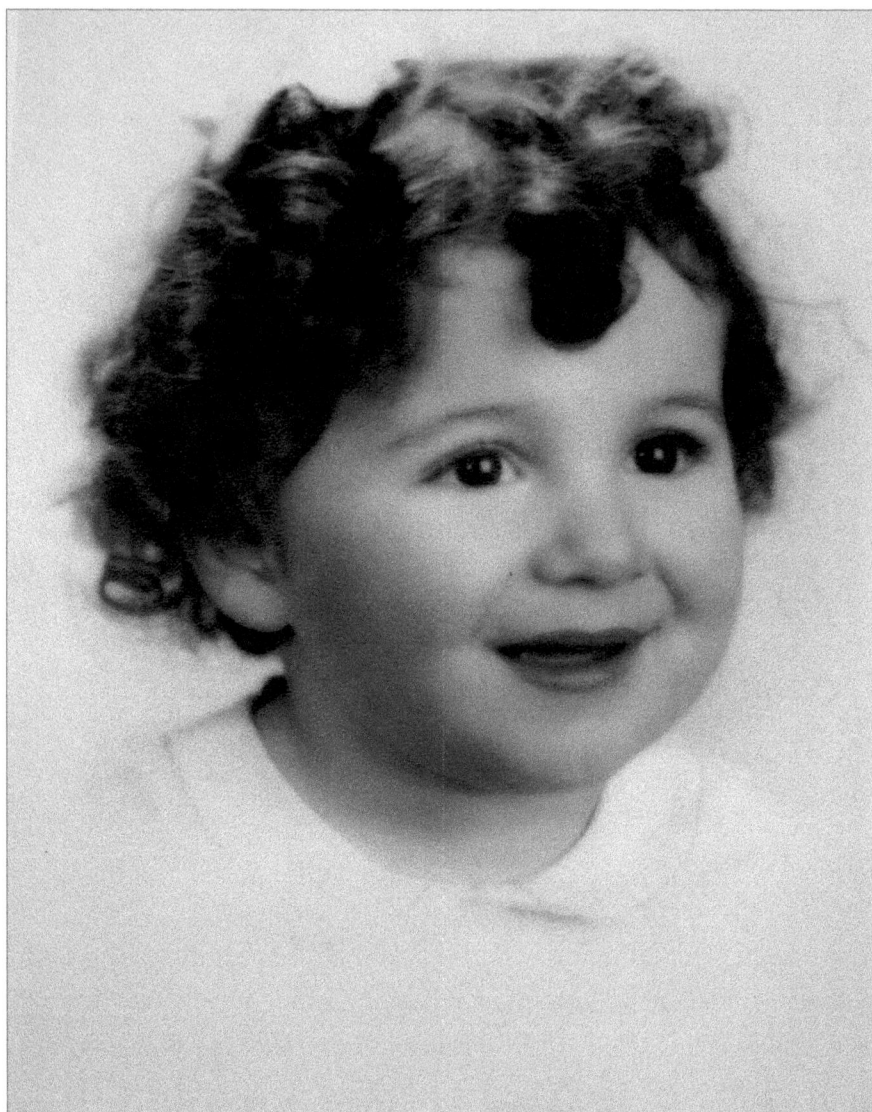

Paula

Contents

A dedication of Love, Joy, and Resilience in this beautiful life

To Sashie, my beloved soul-mate: always, all ways, the splendor of your love holds me, anchors me to this earth plane

To Paula: a deep bow as this heart continues: abundance—a bonne dance

To Mother Ocean: restorative sanctuary, holy water, cosmic rhythm—my spiritual initiation

To Adele and Manuel: birth is holy, chosen, given, received, to taste life: a deep bow, thank you

To the beloveds who share their heartache and joy through conversation and showing up in presence, the work I am privileged to continue

And to the dance, the wondrous dance!

Forever Dance

I am happy even before I have a reason. I am full of Light even before the sky Can greet the sun or the moon. Dear companions, We have been in love with God For so very, very long. What can Hafiz now do but Forever Dance!
—Hafiz

Praise for
Paula Bromberg

Your glorious tome arrived and sits by my bed and I am wading through the introductory pages so much is in these books that I will be wading for a long time. They are very beautiful books with sublime Buddha, the Ocean, and the sublime soul behind it. I feel honored to receive, read and be invited to write comments. Your books and writing are extraordinary, beautiful crafted and I am glad to have The Way of the Lover *and* Notes from the Ocean. *Both are written with such divine perfection. May love and divinity suffuse everything you do. I recommend both of your books to anyone who wishes to live within and be uplifted by the beautiful poetic artistry and heartfelt wisdom of your writing and teaching.*

—Dr. Janine Canan, M.D. poet, Psychiatrist, essayist, story-writer, translator, and editor. Wrote and published 25 books including 5 books/ compilations of the teachings of Guru Mata Amritananda Mayi

Paula's inner processing comes from her own self-exploration and not the reiteration of others thoughts/experiences, but with a need to understand for herself. She has used her devastation to fire her own work. Your book is on our table and has become a daily source of a heart reminder. You have created comprehensive and personal revelations of how you got to where you are. You have thrived, are alive with a soft understanding. You continue to give with your bounty, all you can of your beneficial being. Your light is shining through for any who have tired of darkness, With the highest regard, respect and heartfelt love, I bow.

— Elaine Marchese, Connecticut Book Store Owner

Your book—what a delight! What joy! And wisdom!

> —Carol Donahoe, visual artist living at Paramanhansa
> Yogananda Self-Realization Center Fellowship

I treasure your masterpiece The Way of the Lover and love to read parts of it as soul food when I'm tired of answering thousands of letters. Thank you, thank you, thank you!!! Blessings on the first College/ University based program in this country training hospice workers that we co-created to assist beautiful souls to embrace their transition. Thank you for teaching and writing!

> —Elisabeth Kübler-Ross, M.D., author, psychiatrist, creator of the hospice
> movement, revolutionized the care of the terminally ill, a pioneer in
> near-death studies, inducted into the National Women's Hall of Fame

Paula Bromberg is a genuine big-hearted woman who has a rare and profound intelligence and a deep understanding of authentic compassion.

> —Natalie Goldberg, renowned writing teacher, best-selling author
> of 16 books, painter, retreat leader, filmmaker, zen practitioner

The reminder of Paula's commitment to live her creative potential is what you receive in this book, the culmination of her life work. Paula is connected to the Source, empowering her to live her creative potential. May her journey lead her-lead her-lead her. Her book The Way of the Lover is a true teaching.

> —Edith Wallace, M.D., Ph.D., author, Jungian analyst
> who received her analytic training directly from Carl Jung
> M.D., prize winning painter, world-wide teacher

Dr. Paula is a passionate soul whose vision penetrates the core mystery of what it means to be human.

> —Rabbi Michael Ziegler, founder and leader of Song of Songs
> Minyan, guest faculty Naropa University, book reviewer

In my experience, Paula Bromberg is an extraordinarily knowledgeable Teacher who speaks with the authority of the heart and is gifted with the ability to articulate and clarify her deep understanding of the logos thus making it available to seekers and inquirers.

—José Stevens, Ph.D., international lecturer, psychologist,
corporate team builder, Shaman, author of 20 books

I have known Dr. Paula Bromberg for over 40 years. Thus I have been witness to a magnificent tapestry. Fierce warrior, yet gentle spirit. Seeker, teacher and disciple. The wide eyes and open heart of a child. She teaches us that everything is sacred yet nothing exists. Paula is both illumination and reflection. This book, The Way of the Lover, is a miracle.

—Rona Lieberman, M.D., Physician practicing
responsible medicine for over 35 years.

To aspire towards higher consciousness and spiritual growth defining and understanding one's authentic self is a major component of paramount importance. Dr. Bromberg's book The Way of the Lover is an insightful and informative tool and as a co-companion can guide and support the enfoldment of this learning process, which is ongoing, joyous and eternal. Namaste.

—Mara Howard, yoga and meditation teacher

Paula Bromberg is giftedly willing and able to look at love and all of its expressions with more clarity and honesty than most people would ever dare.

—David Deida, acclaimed author of 10 books, a founder
of Integral Institute, teacher and researcher at University of
California Medical School and École Polytechnique, Paris, France

I have learned much from Paula Bromberg's grasp of human types, as well as her moral sincerity.

—Kabir Helminski, Ph.D., Sufi teacher, psychologist, author and translator of Sufi literature, Shaikh of the Mevlevi order of Sufi which traces to Rumi, tours with the whirling dervishes of Turkey, director of the Threshold Society

Some people write a book in a month and some in a year and others take their time, so the book grows as they do, until we have a living document of a life well-lived and well-considered. Such is this book by Dr. Paula Bromberg, The Way of the Lover, rich in her knowledge, abundant with her wisdom, and redolent with her deep understanding. Socrates said, "The unexamined life is not worth living." Paula's life has been overflowing with self-examination, and through the salient processes she offers, now a significant resource for those who wish to know themselves. Her brilliant opus is a work of art and courage.

Reading Notes from the Ocean, the play of words within words, sounds as music and poetry; teachings about the origin of sound vibrations creating the universe and becoming words. I am enjoying the way music, the ocean, sound soul, the meaning of your name and all the poetry are woven together in Notes from the Ocean. I think of all the studying you have done and feel admiration for what you know and how you put ideas together. You are an amazing woman Paula and have had an extraordinary life. I love the tidbits about your family that come through this book and I must say you have a unique style that's all your own. Thank You.

—Aile Shebar, creative writing teacher, writing coach, editor and author

Notes from the Ocean, A Celebration of Love is an Inspirational Meditation on Love, Life and Song. Dive in. Sing Along!

—Cantor Robert Weiner, Ph.D., Jones Professor of History, Jewish Chaplain Emeritas

Paula Bromberg's The Way of the Lover in clear, simple terms brings tools for self-actualization and empowerment. Bromberg's book is poised to replace conventional psychotherapy and religion as the true journey, the way of choice.

—Larry Chang, author, director of Gnosophia Publishers

Paula Bromberg is a true intellect and a profound healer. Her teaching is magical and has helped me in my work with addicts using a spiritual approach. Deeply rooted in a massive knowledge of people and in life, her book The Way of the Lover is bold and beautiful.

—Kerry Riordan, addiction specialist counselor, New York, Puerto Rico

I have known Paula Bromberg since elementary school days. Both of us traveled healing and spiritual paths. I established a Tibetan Medical Center and Paula became the on-call therapist for my clients in the New York and Massachusetts Centers. A brilliant team—Dr. Paula, Dr. Yeshi Dhonden and Dr. Marsha. Reading her book, The Way of the Lover is like sitting with a master: inspiring, uplifting, educational and enlightening. You must own this book, and carry it around, to actually use. The Way of the Lover fills an important need, finally a guide to understand who we are and how to love.

—Dr. Marsha Woolf, founder and director of New World Medical Center and Alternative Resources, director of Menla Tibetan Medical Institute, author, naturopath, worked for over 25 years with Dr. Yeshi Dhonden, personal senior physician to His Holiness the 14th Dalai Lama

When I write these words about Dr. Paula I want to say thank you. They come straight from my heart with endless gratitude.

Paula Bromberg's book The Way of the Lover is transformational in its nature to understand more of what one refers to as "Self." It is a reference I continue to explore, encouraging me to become more

curious and introspective in my daily life's work and as a yoga practitioner and teacher.

Life unfolds in mysterious, beautiful ways to show us why and how we are living in this lifetime. Paula's guidance to support, transform, encourage, and lift, is a gift I will always hold in the depths of my heart. I have gone to places in my own soul I never imagined, and my love, joy, and gratitude for my life has never felt stronger and content. Paula's personal gift to this lifetime in giving unconditional love, and seeing each individual truly for who they are, has been instrumental to my life's work. Having Paula as a mentor is indescribably precious.

—Meaghan Tozzi, yoga teacher, artist, designer, mother

A life's work
A true understanding of the path
The recognition of the illusion
of our separateness
This is her guide book
and the tools that are needed
to plow the mind
into a vibrational frequency
of the real
Love upon love

—Charles Soloway, Udbodha, musical artist, created *Awakening*

Your book Being Eighty is so lovely—it resonates through me.

—Kim Lerner, co-creator with Rebbe Akiva Mann, Institute for Jewish Knowledge and Learning

When I hear Paula's words from her newest book, Being Eighty, I breathe in and let the words be with me, grateful for the teaching, reading. I am a balloon where the air around me has been filled with a way of being lifting me out of myself into a broader, wider, open heart and a new way of seeing. I embrace Paula's words, hold and digest the sharing of her life and experiences. I am grateful and want to giggle because what a find this book is!

When Notes from the Ocean arrived, I started reading the introduction, 'the Invitation,' and it was. I wanted to tuck the book under my arm and carry it with me wherever I was going. I knew this was a find, it had a similar feeling as to having discovered a wonderful secret and it is. I breathe in gratitude to Paula Bromberg's words. Grateful for her books as they accompany me on this journey in life. Thank you for the gifts.

—Deborah Kane, clinical social worker, photographer, artisan

Dr. Bromberg is a brilliant woman with much insight into the soul. She has been my teacher into how to live in this world. Her book, Being Eighty: A Great Ride, will help anyone aging, through humor and self-knowledge. Enjoy the read.

—Sandi Greenberg Weiner, entrepreneur, business leader, top executive, sales director at Mary Kay, Inc.

Testimonial

The Work Works

Paula challenged me and gave me the courage to step into myself. Throughout the process I learned to truly be in the moment. The joy and freedom I feel is a gift I am grateful for everyday. She saved my life. She gave me my life.

I have worked with Paula for twelve years. Over those years, she challenged me and gave me the courage to be me. In the process I learned to love my nature and respect myself. With her guidance, I had the health, clarity, and energy to raise a beautiful family.

When I hear Paula's voice on the phone I know I am going to be ok. The work isn't always easy, but under her guidance, I have learned to love my nature. I crave her wisdom, clarity, and problem solving. She's both held my hand and kicked me in the butt. Because of Paula, I have been able to raise two beautiful children and keep a marriage strong. I'm also just more joyful, a gift I am grateful for everyday.

—Elizabeth Clair Flood, author, editor, photographer

Just sitting here at sunset, loving you. Hope you feel it. You've given me the greatest gift of my life, which is my life right now in this moment. I hold you in the same regard I hold my birth mother, in total gratitude for giving me an opportunity of a beautiful life. The beauty of my love and life is because of you.

I can never express my deep gratitude because not a day goes by that you don't wander (or firmly roll) into my thoughts. Thank you dear Paula for everything. My life is because of you. I love you now and always, and my children also know your presence because of the way I parent them. A deep exhale and deep bow to you, Paula my beloved mamaji.

—Amanda Botur, yoga teacher, leads yoga teacher trainings, masters in traditional chinese medicine, classical homeopath, songwriter, musician—album *Confluence*

Paula is my sage, a voice to my soul and heart. She has brought a voice to a perspective on myself that I wouldn't have otherwise. I am eternally grateful for her in my life.

Amanda, my wife, introduced me to Dr. Paula as we started working through our stories and problems as a married couple. She has been there through thick and thin, with guidance, compassion, and humor to our individual stories. She has come to our collective defenses and our indifference throughout our 18 years of marriage. Paula has added a strength and significance to bond our family journey.

—Freddie Botur, conservation pioneer and adviser, cowboy, cattle rancher, Cottonwood Ranch, climber and Alpinist, asset manager, entrepreneur

I have worked with other therapists in the past, but none of them enabled me to transcend my history and the pain entangled there in the way that Paula has.

Paula is exceedingly wise and compassionate. Her comprehension of an individual's particular nature, what I understand to be the truth of who a person is beyond her conditioning, is profound. With Paula's gentle yet powerful support I have come to recognize and embrace my true nature and this has given me much relief from suffering as well as enormous peace.

I consider Paula to be a teacher and mentor guiding me on an intimate journey of self-discovery. I am deeply grateful for her in my life.

—Cynthia S. DaCosta, psychotherapist, horse trainer, philanthropic foundation / grant-maker

Paula Bromberg has given me one of the greatest gifts of my life—she gave me back myself. I began working with her over 20 years ago when I was emotionally lost, in unloving relationships, unhappy. Paula, through deep compassion, humor, and pushing me to do my work, helped me peel back the layers and patterns I'd hidden behind for decades. I began to re-discover my true self and, with that, true peace. I am now a joyful person, almost all the time, and even when facing several tragedies at once a few years ago, I knew I would be ok. And I was ok. Because Paula had given me the gift of myself. And isn't that really what we are all searching for? Isn't that where all our life's purposes and work and joy reside?

Paula is both a demanding teacher, always insisting I own every situation, every choice in my life. And never allowing me to blame another. She is also a deeply loving and hilariously funny teacher too. 21 years after meeting her, I still call her whenever there's turmoil in my life and her easy laugh and deep insight make me instantly feel better. Paula's work is so unusual in its depth, but also in its sensitivity. My emotional health doesn't look like my friend's health or my child's health. Paula leads us each to our own mountain top, and each peak is beautiful and each peak is different. She works with me, as me. And maybe most importantly of all, she never loses the connection between health and spirituality. She is grounded and present, but she always gently reminds me that I am part of something much larger than myself. That spiritual connection, coupled with a deep sense of knowing and loving who I am, has created a joy in my life, the depth of which still surprises me. It is resilient, it is generous and it is loving, because when we are connected to our true, healed selves and to the limitless love of the universe, life is beautiful.

Paula has made me rich because I have peace, I have compassion. And I have joy. I will always have profound gratitude and love for her and how she has enriched my life.

—Heather Pentland, L.Ac., created New Leaf Healing Center, trained in China and New Mexico in traditional chinese medicine, acupuncture and herbal medicine

Every week I am grateful for my time with Paula. She has helped me through some of life's most difficult bumps and helped me to feel more calm, grateful and happy. She has helped me parent with more grace and love and to see some of the most beautiful and hidden parts of my children.

Dr. Paula pushes me when I am ready for growth and is gentle and reassuring when I am not. Her influence on my life and my family's life has been an incredible gift.

—Kristen Revill, B.A., Dartmouth College M.A.
Stanford University, currently teaching on the science
faculty at Jackson Hole Community School

Little did I know that when I contacted Dr. Paula Bromberg over 13 years ago how much of an impact on my life that initial call would have. I had sought counseling a few other times in my life so I was not a total stranger to entering therapy. In an hour over the phone, I could see my relationship issues and struggles more clearly. Working with her was different. She was not going to tell me what I thought I wanted or needed to hear. What ensued was a working journey into a better understanding of who I was and seeing why and how I reacted to situations that were presented in my life.

We used the Enneagram and other tools to help me explore and accept my true nature. I slowly began embracing that true nature. Stopped pushing against it and criticizing it. I shifted how I began to see and accept others, celebrating their differences, but keeping myself on course, my true way of being.

On I traveled, staying in the relationship, keeping my professional practice going, navigating my father's death, my mother's illness, and her passing. That brought sibling challenges and how to negotiate what I needed. Each life event brought a chance to work on myself. I moved to another state, creating another phase of life. My beloved dog passed. There were professional challenges and opportunities to shift my business. As I grew and matured my marriage relationship changed and ended. As I enter this new phase of my life, I am forever in deep gratitude to Dr. Paula.

—Marybeth Minter, DVM, classical veterinary homeopath and nutritional counselor, teacher and lecturer, Mariposa veterinary services

Your legacy is every life you've ever touched.

- Maya Angelou -

Prologue

The title arrived as I sat with the reality of moving into my eightieth year and more. Wow, Unimaginable. This body that walked miles and miles no longer navigates with youthful rhythm ease and fluidity. And still, here in the December of my life, so delicious.

Nor did I plan ahead. Still no written will or much savings. No retirement plan or stocks or insurance policy or cemetery or funeral arrangements. Not even a true plan to walk out or to get on a raft and float off to sea.

And here I be—grateful, appreciative, working, writing, going to the beach and opera, attentive to maintain the equilibrium of this perishable body, as well as uncovering the truth of who I be. Not the person I once imagined I was—I discovered that I am quietly inner, private, reclusive, grateful, self-reflective, needing little external stimulus or entertainment. Preferring light and space and seeing the sky and clouds and ocean. Teaching and learning; a lifetime to live the unfolding of the questions that have propelled me forward: and to study, learn and be present.

I love riding the surrey bike on the boardwalk along the ocean—one of the joys of living in South Florida—great exercise and adventures—people smiling and wonderful fresh ocean air. Yes, What a ride this has been and still is!

*My Yiddish Grandmothers, Zlata Bromberg
and Mary Glassman*

Introduction

A story: An elder of a Jewish family was in court on the witness stand. *How old are you?* asked the district attorney. *I am, keyn ahara, eighty-three.* The district attorney asked again: *What was that?* The elder replied, *I am keyn ahara, eighty-three. Just answer the question!* Said the DA sharply. *Nothing else. Now, how old are you? Keyn ahara, eighty-three,* said the elder. Now the judge said: *The witness will answer the question and only the question, without additional comment, or be held in contempt of court.* Up rose the counsel for the defense. *Your honor, may I ask the question?* He turned to the elder: *keyn ahara, how old are you?* Said the elder: *eighty-three.*

How to translate the untranslatable, especially to young people today living impatiently within a quick realm of digital solutions and immediate google answers. Yiddish, colorful filled with innuendos, flavorful and picturesque, levels and shades of meaning, overtones and undertones, satire, wit and humor has been said to be a *tongue that never takes its tongue out of its cheek.*

Jews as well as most Europeans have been linguists out of necessity, so close is one country to another, nearby border crossings have brought a need to adapt to new locations, ultimately most Europeans are proficient in two, three and four languages. And in our American

1

language we have Yiddish phrases sprinkled randomly invading unrecognizably our everyday language.

The official translators of Yiddish, even the erudite ones, always fail. They miss the point and give up on any exact definition, literal or metaphoric. Listen, here's what happened to us; we are not only what happened to us, we are what we will make of it. This language of survivors. Oy a broch! (What a curse, oh a blessing, woe betide me.) Now have a little more chicken soup.
—Rabbi Delphine Horvilleur

Humor, often the heart of Yiddish, displays itself in many forms; jest, sarcasm, irony, ridicule, wordplay, in inflections and attitude, bringing sweetness to bitter times, and so, when asked to translate *keyn ahara* from the German *kein, not one, no,* to the Hebrew, *ayin harah, the evil eye, the evil eye permitting,* how then to capture the essence, the fabric of the world of Yiddish!

Words, like nature, half reveal and half conceal the soul within. —Alfred Lord Tennyson

Many of us remember the years our mother attempted to ward off the evil eye to protect her children, to thwart the mysterious beings out in the atmosphere who sought our demise, especially when there was recognition or praise for her children's virtues, good looks or wealth. This incantation was said to avert misfortune since the spirits are always listening—the air is filled with messengers that are hanging around waiting for someone to say something positive so they can enter and ruin it—and so *keyn ahara* is said to neutralize that. We certainly don't want to tempt fate.

Yiddish sayings are beyond rational explanation. The infinite is beyond understanding. Directed to surrender and live with the grace of blessings, not to provoke the evil eye; invited to live in the wisdom of the what is, to learn what it means to be human.

Since the seventh of October 2023, wherever we find ourselves, whatever situation we face, all languages need to be spoken in Yiddish. Make no mistake: Yiddish isn't the language of Jews. It's the language of all people who see from the depths of despair that their shaky humanity calls out to be saved. —Rabbi Delphine Horvilleur

Our partnership with higher powers is a bridge to become a *mentsch*, an upstanding human being—this is the integrity, opening a door to the physical and spiritual realm.

Words are not just words. They have moods, climates of their own. When a word settles inside you, it brings a different climate to your mind, a different approach, a different vision. —Osho

I grew up in a home where my mother and my father's mother both spoke Yiddish. Mary Glassman and Zlata

Bromberg arriving from what shifted between Russia and Poland, changing as the geographical borders relocated, speaking a language, it is said, *whose precious jewels are undried, unconcealed Jewish tears.* Yiddish was the spoken language for most European Jews for over one hundred years, the *mother tongue, Mamaloshen,* the language of the home and family passed down from mother to child. *Papaloshen, father tongue* is connected to Hebrew; men were primarily engaged in the study of Hebrew texts and liturgy—a reflection of the historical reality—language as influenced by gender roles.

Nobel laureate Isaac Bashevis Singer wrote: *Yiddish has not yet said its last word. The tongue of martyrs and saints, of dreamers—rich in humor, the wise and humble language of us all, the idiom of humanity.* Yiddish, therefore, became the language of the heart, the tongue of the women.

Both of my parents spoke to their mothers in Yiddish and I absorbed the feelings, character and flavor of these two remarkable women into my spirit and heart. I stand on the shoulders of my foremothers and forefathers, a heritage, a foundation from generation to generation; we stand on the shoulders of those before us, their culture, traditions, labor, strength and heartbreak, permeating through time a legacy of love.

Mit simcheh geit men arose fun alleh engshaften. With joy one can overcome distress. —Words of our Sages

Preface

To testify, to bear witness has kept humanity alive. *Yidden, shreibt und fershreibt. Jews, write it down, write it all down*, a directive, from the great Russian-Jewish historian Shimon Dubnov, who, when facing imminent death in the Latvian Riga ghetto, called out to his compatriots in his native Yiddish: *Jews, write everything down;* to leave documents testifying to the lives destroyed, the crimes against humanity.

This determination to bear witness and record our experiences provide invaluable testimonies of resilience and spirit. And Jewish victims of the Holocaust, hiding in bunkers from the Nazis scratched their names into walls, buried manuscripts in tin cans under the ghetto streets so in time their names, their words, their lives might be remembered.

The great force of history comes from the fact that we carry it within us, are unconsciously controlled by it in many ways, and history is present in all that we do. It could scarcely be otherwise, since it is to history that we owe our frames of reference, our identities, and our aspirations.
—James Baldwin

Elie Wiesel stated in his Nobel acceptance speech, *if anything can, it is memory that will save humanity. I am a teacher and a writer, not a politician. When language fails, when there is no communication, the result is violence. This is the reason I teach.*

It is our duty to account and recount to remember, world stories as well as accounting to our particular life story. Not to forget. If we don't know our own story, our history, then the danger is that others define it for us. And so we become chroniclers bearing witness to memoir to our legacy, heritage and traditions. Who will be the voice of memory as we continue? How will we become a moral conscience for this world? How will we become human together? How do we build bridges, uncover our uniqueness and individuality, build souls, stay honest, become a witness?

We are the stories we tell. Stories provide us with identity, meaning, and purpose. Story is how we make sense of the World, and find a place for ourselves within it. The secret to everything is in its story, they are more than memory, they are creative acts of world-making. Our stories define us, instruct us, create us. Without our stories, we do not exist, as the sad plight of amnesia sufferers makes so very clear. For us, our story is our self. Stories transcend time and space. A good storyteller isn't afraid of any story they tell awakening the soul. —Rami Shapiro

This is the reason I teach and continue to have meaningful conversations. This is my effort to write it down. There is an ancient teaching that an eternal beloved spirit puts books into some people, and therefore it is the obligation of these people to give birth to the books they find within themselves.

May the birth of this book, *Being Eighty, Keyn Ahara,* carry meaning and purpose to mine as well as to your life.

Sometimes the right story can change your life.
—Mitchell Chefitz

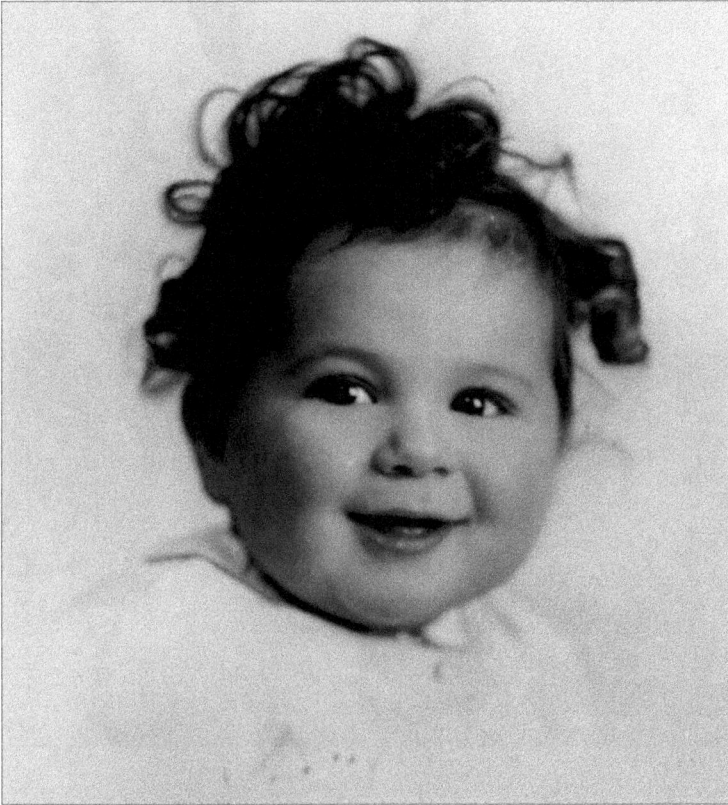

Paula

What a ride!

Section One:
Being Eighty

When my mother was eighty we stopped counting. Each birthday forward became eighties. Now I have become this mother whose body enters eighties with the ease of sliding through the decade—keeping this body afloat, this wobbly aging boat rocking on the river of life appears. I see it in the eyes of the other, *eighty-three, wow, you look great*; meaning, *I am younger and don't really know what eighty looks or feels like.* They surmise eighty as a closing chapter; I see timeless continuity, circular continuation, a small droplet that will one day join the ocean.

Living into my eighties I have under the imprinted youth of personality, discovered a closer connection to the colorations and dispositions of my nature and essence. The privilege of aging and the enthusiasm to investigate brings forth greater refinement and understanding. Asking what do I value to preserve? How to live into cherishing this present moment. What matters? Maintaining the clarity and sharpness of the mind—to use our ordinary life—to come to *real* life; self-reflection—to consciously live in awareness with open heart.

Poet Alan Ginsberg, still relevant today, shook the literary and legal world back in the 50s. To interpret is to impoverish, particularly in a culture that is devoid of deeper meaning. His prophetic poem *Howl* opens with: *I saw the best minds of my generation destroyed by madness, starving hysterical naked.* Ginsberg's tribute to artists, thinkers: the weight and measurement of the world is Love. The wonder is not that we survive and live, it's that from the depths we find, we celebrate, as it is: the spirit of love that enables emboldens uplifts our life. We celebrate the old souls whose lives fall outside what was once considered mainstream, we advocate for those who are marginalized because of their sexuality, race, political ideas considered radical in a country that claims to welcome differences yet fails to protect the rights of the dreamers and the different. Individuality, and yes, everything in this world is holy. Let us have holy living in the simple and ordinary. To never look away: life is both dark and light, grim and joyful, appalling and ter-rific, woeful and blessed, let's stand and sing and dance, let's bow in reverence to everything sacred including those whose minds have become broken, enjailed, over-whelmed with worry and tension until they are discon-nected, eventually absent.

The artist prays by creating. —Flannery O'Connor

Ordinary mind is the way—chop wood, carry water—immediate and direct. Timeless. Let us live as a buddha to consecrate and sanctify the divinity of the simple; we bow to the breath that anchors us.

Preparation for the immense task of remaining conscious through death must be to become intensely conscious of oneself in life. —Rodney Collin

An autobiography is an obituary in serial form with the last installment missing. —Quentin Crisp

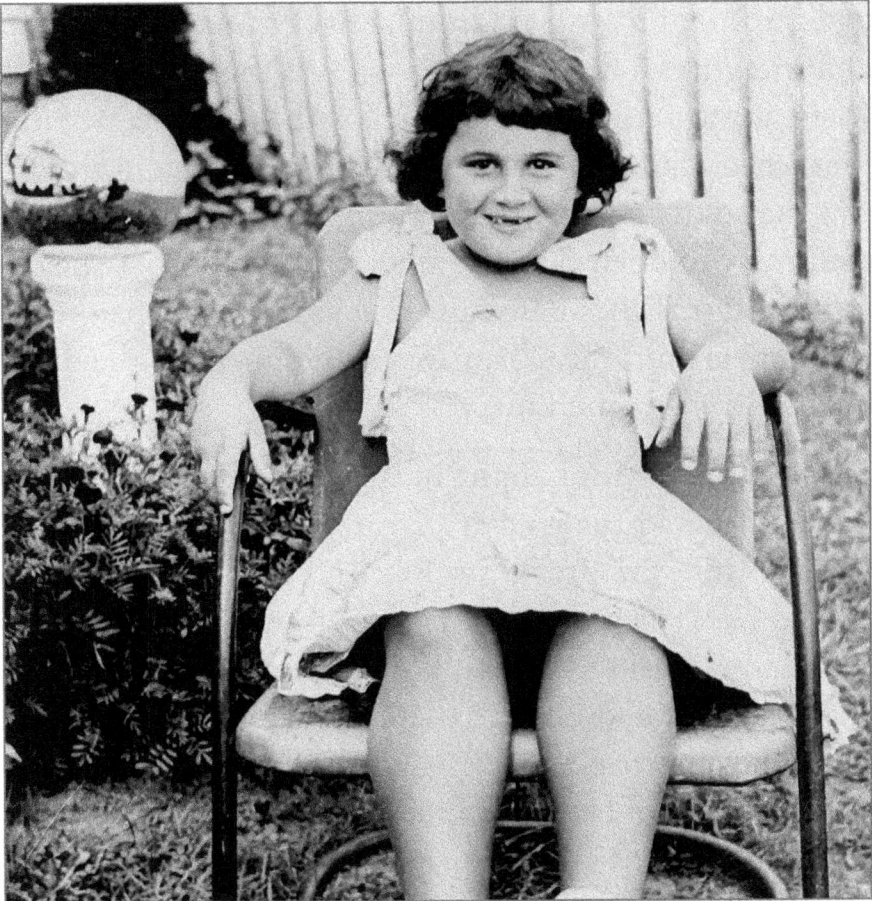

Paula at Narragansett, Rhode Island

Section Two:
A Changeable World

*M*y recent acquaintanceship with a Japanese woman raised a question—why haven't I had Japanese friends especially since I adore a culture so deep and meaningful with traditions that resonate to my life and integrity. Then it clicked—I was raised in a home where it was verboten, forbidden by the higher law of my mother to acknowledge Japan. *They murdered my brother* was the source of the prohibition. My illicit connection continues to open doors revealing a culture that speaks to my heart. Rules based on fear, opinions, separation; misnomers limit the expansiveness required for the open inclusivity we name Love.

The *Aha* I wrote about in my book *The Way of the Lover*, access to the greater picture, story drops away to awaken from the dream, to live into that consciousness named reality, truth, what is eternal within, to become and know who we are, to slide into the conversation between lover and beloved. This gift of finding the treasure takes time and practice, and practice brings us to the possibility of being here now, develops true presence. What a luxurious gift and privilege time is, to experience life as it is. Freed of delusions, illusions, attachments, distractions, addictions; *Hineni*—to say: *here I am!*

The practice is what you throw yourself into.
Unconditionally. The practice is the teacher.
Your *practice is* **your** *teacher.* —Maurine Stuart

Dropping into the what is regardless to the wandering mind's opinions bring us directly into the present moment. The mind remembers what was, to assess and pin us to alter reality. How beautiful: our snow covered head of hair often appearing in the winter of our life becomes a reminder of impermanence and the inevitability of walking towards our destiny. We experience the natural world of shifting seasons, animals nonresistant to their process of life are as is.

Impermanence is limitless, our personal body not so. Nothing lasts, everything lasts, and so the preciousness of each moment strikes a chord, a bell that reverberates, a sand mandala to be wiped away. Sometimes I look strongly into the mirror—this face that beautifully reflects me and here I am. Aged, seasoned, deepened, still beautiful, this aging cherub of light, alive, filled with hope and appreciation for the precious days, still reverberating inviting me to enter more deeply, to become nothing; Nada, empty.

We are like beads strung on a single thread of Love.
—Mata Amritanandamayi

Section Three: Conversation

This being human is a guest house —Rumi

It's summer in South Florida, a time I often sit quietly at the ocean reflecting the endless range of colors, sounds and oxygen in the sea. A young man peered under my umbrella to excitedly point out a sting ray swimming slowly close to the shore. Not notedly aggressive, curious and playful when threatened their instinct is to stop or swim away. *I am going to capture him,* exclaimed the eager young man. I replied: *what if someone entered your home and chased you around and tried to capture you? We are guests of mother ocean which is home for the ray.* A pause of understanding, a smile of recognition and a *thank you* as he slowly moved away and walked to the ocean to enter further south so the ray could peacefully swim away undaunted to freely explore the shallow waters. Words sing and our task is to hear the melody.

Words can sometimes, in moments of grace attain the quality of deeds. —Elie Wiesel

Ah, a conversation, our words express the contents of our heart, this vulnerability, transmission of heart, kindness, carrying us to the ocean of our soul, becoming what

14

we know, the heart is a reflecting mirror; a conversation brings understanding—and understanding is love.

Always remember: Joy is not merely incidental to your spiritual quest. It is vital. Know! The whole world, life, is a narrow bridge. —Rebbe Nachman of Breslov

Section Four:
Stop

Coming or going, always at home. —Zen saying

The struggle of our life is our paradise when we know how to use it, a blessing—a curse when it uses us, *ashrey, happy, content are they,* the good life, a gift when used well. To recognize and see magnificence. To see beauty in one another is seeing our humanity: may we build a world where the beauty in all is honored.

When a form dissolves the empty space is a death and every moment contains a form we lose, the promise is while we experience the formlessness something new is born, and so we focus the heart, this practice of radical equanimity without judgement, this is our practice—to feel the limitlessness of the day and breathe it in. Timeless and impermanent, tenuous and elusive, how to reframe this knowing and regain the wonder: to be present where I am.

In an age of speed, I began to think, nothing could be more invigorating than going slow. In an age of distraction, nothing can feel more luxurious than paying attention. And in an age of constant movement, nothing is more urgent than sitting still. —Pico Iyer

During Covid time I was struck with the image of musical chairs, a game we played as children. When the music stopped we excitedly grabbed/landed on a chair. This is that chair we currently sit on. And still the itch to see if there is a better chair. Maybe the chair could be in New Mexico or upholstered differently, red instead of yellow, placed by a window or a bigger window, or in front of a heater or air-conditioner, in Paris, or big enough for two people to sit on together. And then there's: it makes me sad to sit alone on the chair or it's too close to the next chair or too far away from the chair nearby.

Yikes, how the small mind travels to lock us against a brick wall of ifs and possibilities and then so far from opportunities, blessings and stillness. Ah—where is there to go, beyond, inside where the treasure is. One more workshop, cookie, dollar bill, lover, place to see, car to buy. Is this the continuation we speak of or is this continuing so we dare not get off the treadmill. *Stop the world I want to get off,* sang Anthony Newley, a double entendre, for is this a flat world or a round continuous world and how anyways could we get off?

Ninety-nine percent of all work on self is attitudinal.
—E.J. Gold

Gurdjieff said *STOP and* created an exercise that in the midst of our doing we stop to remember ourself, this fragile non-self that's fully occupied with imagining that what we do is who we are. I am my cookie, I am my

17

car, I am my thoughts and therefore *Life is Real Only Then, When I Am.* And so, we become lifelong seekers, searching for the elusive satisfaction, the enoughness, the magical miraculous moment of capturing the rainbow of stillness, the liberation of the mind.

There is an outer command of stop where we become motionless in a position, what children call *freeze* when they play *Simon Says.* And there is an inner stop where we become motionless in our mind. Thoughts rise and fall, eventually they do not find me. This begins releasing ourself from the prison of our opinions, judgments and criticism.

The day you decide that you are more interested in being aware of your thoughts than you are in the thoughts themselves—that is the day you will find your way out.
—Michael Singer

This is where delight arises, the wonder of being alive. The ultimate truth of this life is this life. And we squirm against the urgency of being present. Impatient for the light to change although we are somewhat colorblind. I sit and watch the ocean color variation even knowing that the ocean is colorless. It's truly the white of all whites reflected from father sky, mother earth, mother moon, sister sun, brother wind. Our ancestral heritage that brings life for I am the daughter, a recipient of this bounty.

Each thought, each action, in the sunlight of awareness, becomes sacred. —Thich Nhat Hahn

Section Five:
Bearing Witness

El Tornillo walks the streets of Melo. People in town think he's crazy He carries a mirror in his hand and he looks at himself with furrowed brow. He doesn't take his eyes off the mirror. 'What are you doing, Tornillo?' 'I'm here,' he says, 'keeping watch on the enemy.'
—Eduardo Galeano

Keeping watch, bearing witness we bring attention to the present moment rather than the wanderings of mind thoughts. Circumstances come and go and yet ultimately nothing prevents old age and dying. The mirror has large brushstrokes—is it in the eyes of the other as we incorporate their glance, their look? Who is our looking glass as we regard the reflection.

My middle name Nada, nothing, is a marvelous reminder of who I am not. A world appears where the remarkable is unremarkable. Coming or going, always at home is a well treasured posture of being in this life. Beyond preoccupation with the self, there is a world out there. In the absence of entertainment and distractions, without television or parties or group gatherings, minus visiting people or having anyone stop by, without telephone conversations where the other lists their daily routines or tales about their children, what is left when the clutter diminishes and only the impulse, minus thought, arises. Here and now to be in tune with the harmony of this very moment, this very body the buddha.

Years lived brings me to knowing that anything outside my own thoughts are an illusion. Nothing outside to blame or hold accountable, a spiritual warrior is soft, tender, knows there is nothing to control, only to live courageously alive.

Waking up to who you are requires letting go of who you imagine yourself to be. —Alan Watts

I remember getting off a bus on Sixth Avenue in Manhattan and quickly crossing Nineteenth Street when the side mirror on a Ryder truck smashed into my head. A narrow thread between reality and an opening that brought me to a life teacher who made jokes about how I needed to have a truck hit me in the head before I could truly see. The miracle of the truck moved me into an awareness of my lack of presence and connection as I hurriedly traveled through life not paying attention as a huge yellow Ryder truck barreled towards me. What bring us to inwardly stop?

Each and every one of us was raised in a palace surrounded by walls. In those very things that we most deny lies the greatest energy for healing. But first we must bear witness: to AIDS, to poverty, to hunger. To

rivers, to mountains, to a laughing child. To war, to
Auschwitz, to the morning star. By saying, 'This is me.'
—Bernie Glassman

I recall driving cross country from New York heading to New Mexico hitting black ice in Arkansas as I drove across a metal-lined bridge. My car catapulted, flung itself into the air and down a ravine. These life accidents, a moment in time, chase us throughout our life, sometimes called fate, other times destiny. We bear witness to the impactful irreversible situations not to let them crush us. No solid ground under us.

Too young for there to be a witness when the accidents happen early on. Two and a half years old and a wire from a stuffed bunny penetrated my eye. Five years of age in bed with scarlet fever, isolated; to decontaminate the house, to disinfect my room, all my toys and books removed from the house to be burned to prevent the disease from spreading. Without an observer how do we file this information to later be of service to our awakening; in childhood we have lived in a twilight zone. My mothers red ribbon over her child's bed did it bear witness?

Life changing, to testify to life as it unfolds. Buddha placed mindfulness at the heart of all teaching. These invisible connections weaving throughout our life begin to offer understanding as we weather and age. We study this instrument called self to be at home as the driver, the one who knows and is behind the wheel called mind is where to place our attention as Tornillo continuing to walk through a world of thorns and roses. Life is a practice towards waking up and each incident a reminder of impermanence, the fragility of the body, all grist for the mill. Inquiry takes courage, manages the precariousness of life. Life is the teacher, our initiation and experiences teach us, serve us as we recognize the inherent privilege of aliveness.

If memory is to make a moral difference, we need to locate ourselves within it. It is not enough to know the facts. We must take things—history, current events—personally. We must look in mirrors. And great literature can act as a mirror. Great books, like mirrors, can serve as tools of self-awareness.
—Elie Wiesel

These gifts repeatedly presenting themselves, often seen as impediments, woundings, initiations, windows into a life that aging allows us to peer through, piece and weave together, use as teachings. To know that: *Our wound is the place where the Self finds entry into us,* are we willing to bear witness!

Remember, hold still and see. Look into the mirror of the heart as the inner eye opens to see light everywhere. Now we see the visible manifestations of the invisible. A lucky lifetime to witness, indeed!

You've no idea
how hard I've looked
for a gift to bring You.
Nothing seemed right.
What's the point of bringing
gold to the gold mine,
or water to the Ocean.
Everything I came up with was
like taking spices to the Orient.
It's no good giving
my heart and my soul
because you already have these.
So
I've brought you a mirror.
Look at yourself and
remember me.

-Rumi

Section Six:
Sound or Sight

Being blind is having sight but no vision.
—Helen Keller

*I*well remember the conversation with my sister-in-law Marcia years after her brain aneurism. *Which would you rather have—your hearing or your sight?* asked Marcia. And I would shift my attention from the great joy I receive from listening to music and happiness with a good conversation to the visual aesthetic nurturance I receive from seeing colors and movement, even from looking at the spaciousness of the horizon and clouds and sky. I cherish seeing beauty whether it's catching a small child smiling or seeing my beautiful beloved enter a room.

Eventually Marcia, struggling to hold on to any remnant of sound or sight, had both her senses diminished to barely any sound or sight. Internal isolation restful or stressful? And today, for me it's vision I cherish, even still having no hearing in my left ear which also is occupied with the near constant tinitus sounds. And, yes, there is only the question—I no longer expect an answer. That arises through living, through regarding comings and goings.

The greatest gift ever offered is not the gift of sight but the gift of vision. Sight is a function of the eyes, vision is a function of the heart. —Myles Monroe

The ocean waves taught me these magnificent truths; she welcomes all her phases, the currents moving rhythm, untamed magic, salt water and air, powerful and allowing, shapeless and unpredictable, both welcoming and forbidding. Without opinion all our phases, such is the nature of a life well-lived. Not standing in the way is the foundation of our practice.

Kindness is a language that the deaf can hear and the blind can see. —Mark Twain

Aging oftentimes diminishes visual clarity, the sharpness of the world, colors remain clear, shapes lose their hard edges. Moving through my eighties I continue to drive, more carefully, not as well defined at night; there are less places to go—what is there to see now that entertainment, shopping and distractions have lost their glamour. Inner vision carries a wealth of imagination.

My 98-year-old cousin Henry often laughs saying: *the parts wear out,* although nowadays many of our bodily parts are replaceable. He happily puts his hearing aid in before we go out to a restaurant, and sports a pacemaker, new heart valves and shoulder replacement. In many ways we are blessed to be alive in modern times of western medicine that can update our physical hard drive.

And what transcends physical limitations: deaf people see their thoughts in pictures, in images and signs. Touch and sound and light perception are often in the field of vision, and Marcia retained this adaptation as she continued to move around in her world.

These essential functions, easily taken for granted when we have them, often diminish with the aging process. Each sense—sight, sound, taste, smell, vestibular (balance and spatial orientation), proprioception (body awareness), intuition, knowing/awareness (understanding); all our senses enhance living and the ability to connect and interact with the world.

Aging I continue to prioritize, and on one hand the dominant source that provides the most information has been considered to be vision, the fastest sense for processing information. Marcia lost her sense of sight, hearing, smell and taste, while maintaining her sense of understanding—of creating meaning from information. The convergence of my senses have brought me to learn that our seventh sense of awareness, looking beyond the narrative thread, is the freedom to continue, to let all matters take their course, called mindless mind. Metacognition, the awareness of one's mental processes, the capacity to reflect, awareness. This is unity consciousness—greater than the sum of its parts. This appears to create the human—awareness, the ability to know, remember and be present. Gratitude to ordinary experience, the beauty of love, to be alive and present.

There is a life force within your soul, be that life. There is a gem in the mountain of your body, be that mine. Look inside and be that. —Rumi

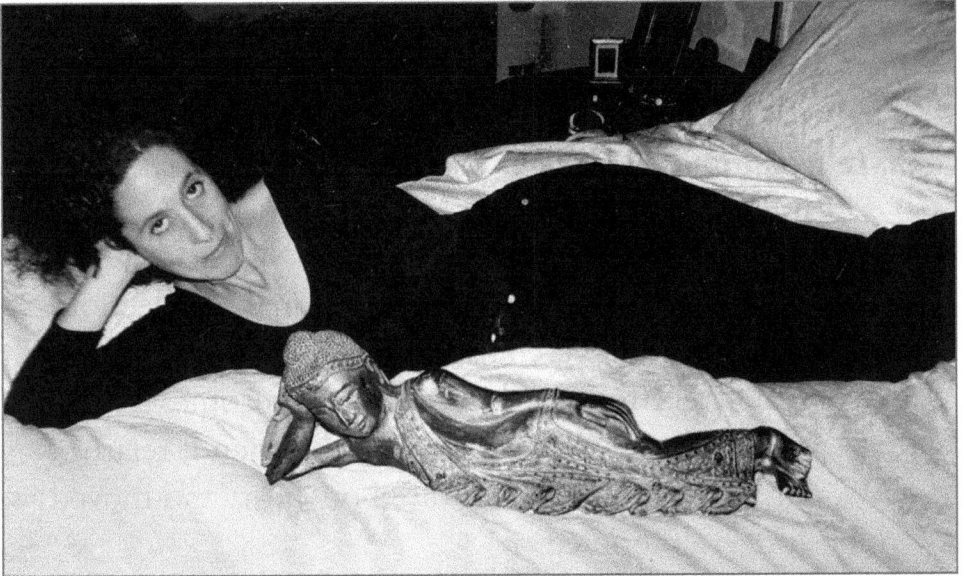

Section Seven:
Memory

We have to relearn the art of resting. Even when we have a vacation, we don't know how to make use of it. Very often we are more tired after a vacation than before it. We might learn the art of relaxation and resting. and make some time each day to practice deep relaxation.
—Thich Nhat Hahn

My early years of childhood personal recollection, memories, were absent. Now aging, memories arrive with little effort. Each recollection becomes a sanctuary, a holy place with reverence to the friend, relative, child, dog, those who have captured my heart and moved on, no longer embodied.

My sister, Iris, struggles to retain her memory, her location. *Dementia,* she said the doctor calls it. A diagnosis. Fate, lifestyle, destiny, death sentence. I have felt sadness as she struggles to recall—to locate herself. Iris ridiculed me my whole life for any effort I made to look more deeply at life. *Stop! Don't analyze,* she admonished me with words that wounded, that created separation, as she made fun of how I saw the world. Iris preferred to skim the surface, to investigate others secretly, suspiciously. The mind—can she catch hers as thoughts wander away. She lives in a memory care unit in Orchard Cove in Canton, Massachusetts. *Confused*, she tells me through the phone line *even more confused at night.* I am the little sister unable to help my big sister. I listen, to possibly comfort. I don't know. No answers. I listen. This is a harsh world: to see suffering. To be human is to ask questions. Questions can save us from the certainties that lead to delusion. To inquire is to unmask, to live with discomfort, to witness with compassion.

Let everything happen to you; Beauty and terror; Just keep going: No feeling is final. Don't let yourself lose me. Nearby is the country they call life. You will know it by its seriousness. Give me your hand. —Rainer Maria Rilke

Tonight at a theatre performance a woman collapsed. Lay on the floor until the ambulance arrived. I remember seeing a man collapse on Fourteen Street in Manhattan many years ago and I recalled that my father had a heart attack in the men's room at Kennedy airport, dying in the ambulance taking him to the hospital. Brought to a morgue, my uncle Leonard was given the task to identify the body before it was transported to Providence, Rhode Island. So fragile the body, unknown who will be by our side, sometimes an emergency medical person, or a passerby, a neighbor, here we are; reach out for connection!

Don't throw your suffering away. Use it. Your suffering is the compost that gives you the understanding to nourish your happiness and the happiness of others.
—Thich Nhat Hanh

When I moved to Fort Lauderdale, Florida, a woman in the next house struggled to put her large rolling plastic garbage pail out in front of her house on pick-up day. I knocked on her door to offer assistance and learned that she was living alone, home with terminal cancer. She was appreciative of the offer. I went by regularly bringing flowers in a vase and sometimes food. Yes, walking each other home, here we are strangers until we are not. Where is the comfort to be found?

It is not the end of the physical body that should worry us. Rather, our concerns must be to live while we're alive— to release our inner selves from the spiritual death that comes with living behind a facade designed to conform to external definitions of who and what we are.
—Dr. Elisabeth Kubler-Ross

When my father died I ate chocolate pudding. Through the mourning. Again and again. Through stomach aches and intestinal pain. I was young. I sat next to my mother while we sat shiva until my high school friend Marsha Woolf came to our house in Cranston, Rhode Island and ushered me out of the room so she could sit in the chair next to my mother as if she were me. I went into a private bedroom to be away from the people, to gather myself, to be alone, to sit quietly with myself.

Not to transmit an experience is to betray it, this is what tradition teaches us, forgetfulness leads to exile, memory to redemption. If anything can, it is memory that will save humanity, said Elie Wiesel, and, so I write as witness, having paid dearly through being ostracized, saying what I saw, dressing as I chose, yearning to wake up, shake up, move mountains. The family I grew up in was speechless, no investigation to meaning, hidden. I remember reading Ionesco's *The Chairs* early on, my first year at Emerson College. A play confronting loss to experience the absence and to include with generosity what was already lost. And the difficulty, contradiction, ambiguity of communication.

A false teaching comforts; a true teaching disturbs.
—Elie Wiesel

How do we exercise this looking, this linking people together: through telling our stories we are witness as we stand on what we would like to perceive as solid ground, not to be the center of the story, rather to hold each other up. And so my life has been dedicated to listening, to not turn away, to meet the world, to show up, to sing and celebrate.

How can you sing? How can you not. —Elie Wiesel

31

The polished heart becomes an unceasing timeless state of self-remembrance. We are not in love, we become love, as a seed becomes a flower. A spiritual communion, finally to love another truly, considered to be the highest experience on earth. This path of love demands commitment, mindful devotion, presence. When we become like a flower in a garden, all who pass receive our lingering fragrance.

Death is a vast mystery, but there are two things we can say about it: It is absolutely certain that we will die, and it is uncertain when or how we will die. The only surety we have then, is this uncertainty about the hour of our death, which we seize on as an excuse to postpone facing death directly. We are like children who cover their eyes in a game of hide-and-seek and think that no one can see us. —Sogyal Rinpoche

Section Eight:
We Rise

This is love: to fly toward a secret sky to cause a hundred veils to fall each moment. First, to let go of life. In the end, to take a step without feet; To regard this world as invisible, and to disregard what appears to be the self. Heart, I said, what a gift it has been to enter this circle of lovers, to see beyond seeing itself, to reach and feel within the breast. —Rumi

Indian born British American novelist Sir Salman Rushdie and the incarcerated African statesman Nelson Mandela both achieved freedom through living internally as free men, not allowing a legal decree hanging over them to hinder their inner journey. Mandela thrived after spending twenty-seven years in jail to become the first president of the new democratic nation, South Africa. Their names forever etched in the story of human rights, inspiring the world through their persistent confidence in justice, forgiveness, equality and reconciliation.

Rushdie living under a 1989 decreed fatwa from the Ayatollah Khomeini was condemned to death for alleged blasphemy in his novel *The Satanic Verses,* which was never rescinded; a singular dictum passed down asking for his assassination.

In 2022 in Western New York the seventy five-year-old Rushdie was stabbed multiple times on stage as he prepared to give a lecture. From this dire circumstance a new book—*Knife: Meditations After an Attempted Murder*, the attack that severed, blinded his eye. Sir Salmon's wife, seeing through eyes of love and compassionate kindness said: *I love his single eye even more because of how he sees the world.*

How do we use our life, is it to be consumed by the dysfunctional family, the compromised political structures, the oftentimes immoral society with unnecessary rules and requirements that frame our life, the ones we are coerced into. How to use the circumstances of this life, to bear witness to the sufferings as well as the joys, the endless possibilities and meet both with courage, resilience, hope, compassion and fortitude to actualize all and everything through practice, our service. We are active agents able to create change in the world. This is our agency and task: not to complete, yet to bring about a world that serves the heart, that celebrates lovingkindness. Quite a task and responsibility!

It is illegal to shout 'Fire' in a crowded theatre.
But if there is a fire, it is immoral to remain silent.
—Elie Wiesel

To be a Bodhisattva offering wisdom and heart, to meet/to witness the suffering, this is where we practice. Looking to those who rise from the flames of hardship, who rise like Don Quixote de la Mancha the knight-errant to revive chivalry; we give voice to diverse perspectives, never abandoning hope. Faith in this world, carrying our brokenness with dignity as part of our journey, our memory, refusing to give up, to meet the world with courage, compassion and wisdom: this is what is asked as we live into our highest self, regardless to circumstances.

Dear, they have dropped the knife. They have dropped the cruel knife that most so often use upon their tender self and others...I have found the power to say no to any actions that might harm myself or another.
—Hafiz

We live in a formitory world of titles, labels, opinions, encouraged to identify with our assumptions, preferences, beliefs, sentiments and thoughts. And yet! Not to go towards heartache, nor to move away. The treasure lies in being still and present. Once one with love we radiate true peace. Choosing to live with our heart open, regardless, we expand our world view, now with compassionate kindness. We rise. In silence with extended arms living connected in courage with a willingness to be the broken openness, the tears that water mother ocean. It is in our hands as we create the future we envision for coming generations.

Nothing can dim the light which shines from within. But still, like dust, I'll rise. My wish for you is that you continue, continue to be who you and how you are, to astonish a mean world with your acts of kindness.
—Maya Angelou

Section Nine:
Our Sanctuary

A whole generation worked to empower women, but forgot to teach men how to live with empowered women.
—Vanshita

Our culture does not provide a sanctuary for us to live in our vulnerability, particularly when we make choices that blur societal rules. So many times I have been told *if you do this then everyone will want to do it*, all to justify a resounding rigidity of no. From renting a beach umbrella and requesting to place it close to the ocean as the tide's receding, to parking under the building where I reside during the weekend while the workers aren't present and the building is under construction. To live in this fractured culture and remain vulnerable, self-contained, open, freed of blaming or pointing a finger outwards requires long consistent practice.

We live in a world peopled with an illusion that daily life has a fairness, as we are raised with a false premise of sharing and being fair. Equal time, parents and grandparents in their efforts to be nonpartisan, unbiased, dole out equal portions and gifts for each child, and then we grow aghast that the other person isn't sharing, mumbling the mantra *it isn't fair,* keeping us from tasting our personal experience of life and other peoples lives with challenges that continuously arrive. How to allow disappointment and trust into our life space, and turn towards courage to participate fully in this world of possibilities? Wounded we continue in the conversation of life as it is, bolstering our immune system through knowing that this very ground we stand on is holy.

I volunteer at an annual event, a naturist children's camp that brings children to a day of swimming and picnicking at the local beach where I have served for over twenty-five years as a beach ambassador. Service to mother ocean's community. For me it's a teaching, to be included in the open-hearted magical adventures of children as they play and laugh and cavort freely on sand and in ocean. The kids brought no digital, no cell phones or iPads—and great fun we all had.

The ocean can do craziness, it can do smooth it can lie down like silk breathing or toss havoc shoreward; it can give gifts or withhold all; it can rise, ebb, froth like an incoming frenzy of fountains, or it can sweet-talk entirely. As I can too, and so, no doubt, can you, and you.
—Mary Oliver

Our true nature is like the sky, its love and wisdom unaffected by the clouds of life. This is our sanctuary, our utmost refuge. How to disengage from narrow confinement, the delusion and entanglement we are caught up in, to allow the obstructions to float away and become a walking path to higher ground, to re-examine all we are told, in the light of hope. True practice is necessary to live purposefully. Awareness itself does not come and go, it pierces through all. The privilege of aliveness, this sacred human life brings us opportunity to realize our own pristine nature and awaken out of the sleep of ignorance.

The Place where you are standing is holy. —Exodus

A child is radiance, is sunlight, and their happiness their sense of wonder and earnest surprise, their genuine curiosity is contagious to be around. For me, a reminder of the essence and undercurrent of my own true nature. A day on the beach in the ocean with the children always a refreshment of aliveness, a mirror to presence. This liquid sea a gateway to quench our thirst to reveal the true value of this precious life.

What is this precious love and laughter Budding in
our hearts? It is the glorious sound of a soul waking up!
—Hafiz

Section Ten:
Building a Bridge to Self

Old, torn and patched is an honest place to begin
without silly illusions and some healthy experience.
—Jean Robertson

Time. I was offered a directive by a Gurdjieff teacher, JR, more than 35 years ago, to go to the desert. Taken literally I saw the vastness of the New Mexico desert, deeper is to know the empty spaciousness as sky, ocean, quieted mind—all desert. To make friends with the desert of this mind. Most experiences take years of digesting: this amazing privilege of aging into the eighties an opportunity to appreciate life slowly, to discover what truly matters.

The teaching Jean transmitted continues through the discovery that living in Florida, peopled with innumerable younger souls imposing rigid rules, who value financial success—money, power, looks and prestige, in fact often placing financial gain above personal and moral integrity, stillness and authenticity, clearly became my desert.

The aridity of invisibility in a world of conforming pressures disregarding true courage and integrity; lacking intimacy with the daily moment offers little solace. Little individuality, life is movement—everything is becoming.

40

Years of being in Florida, gaining a modicum of harmony through repeated beach visits, and yet not seeing how this was the desert—uninterrupted noise, boom boxes, beer bottles on the beach, traffic with careless drivers on roads and highways, people moving pell mell to the malls, restaurants, shopping centers. I let the externals fall away to drop into the aridity, mental sterility, the young soul commonplaceness, until I experienced groundedness, balance. And so the soil has become rich for this growing, and here I am.

Love comes with a knife. You have been walking the ocean's edge, holding up your robes to keep them dry. You must dive naked under and deeper under, a thousand times deeper. Love flows down. —Rumi

Writing is one of the deepest ways that I assimilate, consider, absorb and understand experience, digest my life. To become aware of the contradictions, to eliminate the drama, to be in the experience each moment, to go beyond the story. To be in my heart, a recognition that I am an active agent creating change in this world, to create a world that's celebratory, a world that is so unremarkable that it's remarkable.

Going nowhere, as Leonard Cohen would later emphasize for me, isn't about turning your back on the world; it's about stepping away now and then so that you can see the world more clearly and love it more deeply. —Pico Iyer

I have lived outside the bounds of society most of my life—for fifty-three years and continuing in not a conventional marriage, nor a typical beach my beloved Haulover Beach, voted the number one naturist beach in the world. An unusual book: *The Way of the Lover* a book of 1527 pages—daunting for most, as I am daunting for most. How to be invisible as such a large presence that I am. A lifetime it has taken for me to see and understand this nature that I chose to incarnate as. Quietly, I have worked for the past sixty years as a psychologist/ teacher/ conversationalist/writer: in dialogue with all that is—people, ocean, sky, the songs of life.

My so called favorite name has been *Dr. Funny* by a cherished client labeled with Asperger syndrome. And how is it we connect heart to heart with those who are in our love collective, our circle of beloveds? Open. Language is often used to label and tear apart. A language of unity builds bridges, not fractures. A sense of humor to play, a great enjoyment music, to see with fresh new eyes, and a seat in the clouds on my eleventh floor home.

The first initiation into self-knowledge is to learn to see, but we will see that this is not easy. And it is not cheap. We must pay dearly. We must pay a lot, and pay immediately, pay in advance. Pay with ourself, by sincere conscientious, disinterested efforts. The more we are prepared to pay without economizing, without cheating, without any falsification, the more we will receive.
—Jeanne de Salzmann

Section Eleven:
Question the Unquestionable

Be patient toward all that is unsolved in your heart and try to love the questions themselves, like locked rooms and books that are now written in a very foreign tongue. Do not now seek the answers, which cannot be given you because you would not be able to live them. And the point is, to live everything. Live the questions now. Perhaps you will then gradually, without noticing it, live along some distant day into the answer.
—Rainer Maria Rilke

As a child I lived in the questions, daring to speak what I saw. Satisfaction with glib answers and platitudes was and still is not where I live, there was more to unravel deeper places to live into, further to travel. Dialogue, connection, understanding: the integrity of investigation, the curiosity and wonder did and still brings me to the blessings.

Adults were bewildered by a small child's recognition of the incongruities, uncertainty and contradictions of family life. Certainly my family and school tried to muzzle me, to no avail. I questioned the unquestionable. What is conscience? The meaning of friendship? Integrity? How to engage with the other? Moral clarity? A real conversation? Relentless, unwilling to perform, unassailed by judgments of right-wrong, good-bad; a large presence.

I trusted that there would be an immense love that would embrace me and for years I prayed for that as my fortune and destiny. I imagined that when childhood is difficult the reward would be easer in the later chapters of life. Underestimated, the desire to connect, I knew early on that to connect is to listen and pay attention to how each person experiences the world.

As a child I was interested in the conversation of the adults. Constantly hushed I continued to seek and ask, to question: this was my practice from the earliest age, not silenced by glib answers, wanting time to be playful, to invite others into my heart, I opened into the questions, minus the logistics and drama; through direct experience I opened.

Family and most adults were bewildered, not wanting their reality questioned. In the small world where I was raised most adults were resistant to thinking beyond the surface, to see a bigger picture, to be with things as they truly are, to feel the miraculous. Living in a world where adults often have forgotten the mystery while compromising true happiness; now, let us remember to be happy, to love.

Children live in wonder and amazement, uncertainty, the let's see what wants to happen, not tripped up by the world of unanswerable questions. Each of us with our uniqueness, diversity is our strength feeding unity—truth is the interconnectedness of all life.

Professor Elie Wiesel would enter his classroom at Boston University with a smile and say: *Good morning. Let us begin With your questions.* The power and importance of asking questions is crucial for understanding difficult truths. Questions unite people, answers often divide: shared inquiry is a bridge for authentic connection. *Every question possesses a power that is lost in the answer,* said Wiesel. Engaging in dialogue and exploring together fosters connection. Asking questions is a way to create accountability. Let us continue to look, to inquire, to be responsible. *The essential questions have no answers. You are my question, and I am yours—and then there is dialogue. The moment we have answers there is no dialogue,* said Wiesel. We live in a world where easy simplistic answers set up distance and keep us from meeting each other in that tender intimacy so many of us yearn for.

Fun a kasha shtarbt man nisht, old beloved Yiddish proverb that says: *from a question, no one has ever died.*

The Baal Shem Tov taught that once you enter the heavenly court, because here on earth no one is able to judge your life, you are shown a person's life, their accomplishment, their shortcomings, their wise decisions and the poor choices, then you are asked: *what is it we should do with this person?* You offer the verdict, and it is accepted. Now you are told that this someone is you.

45

Once entering heaven you don't remember. Those who judge favorably have a great advantage. Life is our place of practice; we are here to learn impermanence with soft, gentle, sweet, favorable and easy loving kindness and determination.

A gem is not polished without rubbing, nor a person perfected without trials. —Proverb

❧

And did you get what you wanted from this life,
even so? I did. And what did you want?
To call myself beloved, to feel myself on the earth.
—R. Carver

Section Twelve:
The Light of Holiness

I have, for the years following the death of my mother resisted throwing away certain of her belongings, they carry personality and meaning and I have personified them to sustain life and connection. Yes, everything is connected, nothing lasts, yet our gentle kindness towards our belongings brings meaning and life to the energy that lives within each physical object.

My Japanese friend Hitomi explained to me that when she would kick a door her parents would ask her to apologize to the door, that it too has feelings. Sanibel beaches in Florida visitors are strongly discouraged from removing sand dollars from the beach since they are an important part of the local ecosystem. They are living creatures and there are notices asking people to gently place the sand dollar back in the water near where you found it. To see the life and energy that lives in all living beings and inanimate things is a reminder of our humanity. We all share the same earth and our responsibility to care for our planet, our home, brings everything to life. Maturity is compassionate generosity.

My books warm my heart, the statues in my home uplift; many of the adornments—gifts I have received, are relationships to maintain the givers aliveness.

Paintings from beloved Bonnie, photographs mailed to me from artist clients, plants in beautiful plant-holders from a friend who recently died, energy that vibrates and circulates loving-kindness. Tibetan singing bowls over hundreds of years aged: one extraordinary bowl from my friend Udbodha, several from a dear acquaintance Gisela, notebooks filled with my writings, a hand-built polished granite desk with her cherry wood oversized cabinets, the large oak carefully designed bookcase lining the entire wall. I carefully chose the wood from a lumber yard in Santa Fe, New Mexico for each shelf; all treasures. And still we leave.

There are certain times when I choose to wear my mother's engagement ring, a beautiful diamond ring in the shape of a rose, or my grandmothers vintage art deco diamond ring that holds me tenderly when I look at my hand, my father's gold coin cuff link set in a figaro chain bracelet, memories of passing generations, a living link and connection, a conversation between my foremothers and myself that I carry and imbue with tenderness. Rich. I am a billionaire carrying priceless memories. Valuable beyond estimation.

Om gate gateparagate parasamgate bodhi svada. Gone, gone, gone beyond, completely exposed, awake, so be it.
—The Heart Sutra

The Baal Shem Tov teaches that when things/ possessions are lost, stolen, removed, given away, the light of holiness that was intended as your purpose has been redeemed and your spiritual attachment is lifted. The material is now on to new ownership. And so time continues.

Guggenheim fellowship, writing teacher at Harvard University, Pico Iyer, author especially known for his writing on explorations both inner and outer, as his home burned in Santa Barbara, California grabbed his cat got into a van and raced down the mountain road. By dawn next day everything was gone. Pico quoting a poem by Basho, the 17th century Japanese wanderer, who described releasing belongings, since even destruction sometimes brings clarity: *My house burned down. Now I can better see the rising moon.*

All the same. Keeping and releasing. Ephemeral, fleeting, transient, eternal, imperishable, perpetual, continuing. Joy and grief, is there a difference?

How do we lift up the world of our words. A conversation between ourselves and the world. And words shape reality, they plant seeds.

Pico said: *Home is what you take for granted, and I like that I can't take anything for granted. To an extent, so much of the world is a burning house, the question is: what do we do with the ashes? After all, once you attach yourself to a particular place, it becomes difficult to view that place objectively. Luxury is all the things we can do without. The fire was a humbling experience.*

Extend that to possessions, to things, to people. Once we become sentimental to our belongings and to past relationships we become myopic about true value and the meaning that might be violating or enhancing space in our home, in our life. A delicate dance of sentiment and sensibility.

How to convey the beauty of a past world. We move beyond words, transmitting memories, keeping those souls alive, they are present like the dead are present; souls flicker when I light a yizkor candle repeating a beloveds name. Adele is present when I wear her engagement ring, striking an eight hundred year old Tibetan singing bowl the prayers that monks chanted into the bowl are released to vibrate throughout my home. This requires, demands intention. To keep ourselves fresh is to refresh our external world for there to be space for our internal world, and space is consciousness.

Practice living in a state of unknowing, not of knowing. This is very, very hard since we believe that the way to become more effective is to know more. Developing the openness to see things as they are. Whenever you know, you've reached a dead end. At the same time that we accumulate knowledge and experience, we need to wipe the slate clean and be in a state of unknowing. For only then can we bear witness. —Bernie Glassman

Section Thirteen:
We Are Reborn in Each Breath

If people can't write well, they cannot think well.
And if they cannot think well, others will do their
thinking for them. —George Orwell

My Teacher, Jean, would proclaim: *Thinking is stinking.* The image remains with me. We learn from our teachers and teachings, what they initiate continues for years permeating cellularly, seeds watered eventually grow. The fickleness of the untrained mind teaches us not to think excessively. To taste the moment without the mind, the conjurer who creates illusions, is to liberate ourselves from these rotating thoughts. Mind is a flux, as we quiet, not doing anything particularly, to be here beyond the limited existence of the mind until we enter the mindless mind released from its limitations. *Who am I standing in the midst of this thought traffic?* Asked Rumi. The persistent thoughts, our habits that stand in the way of awareness interrupt our ability to serve and live into a higher realm.

The one who is firmly established in the heart is no
longer distracted by the incessant movements of the mind.
—Mooji

Conversations/dialogue have been a powerful mode for me to digest this life, along with the conversations I have while writing, the ones from the invisible Paula as I lift up the world of words. And the spoken word— from the concealed to the revealed. Our culture does not support vulnerability. How to live open, enthusiastically carrying the spirit of the children is the aspiration.

I moved to South Florida to be with Adele, my mother. Purchasing a home on the water I moved her from the golf course where her apartment was located miles west in Fort Lauderdale, Florida, east to my home by the ocean in Hallandale Beach, Florida. I truly needed the air and ozone that ocean carries. That was a special time to live with the physical source of my life, to get to know the woman who birthed me. A privilege to caretake and live with the mother who took care of me as a child. Always new, love flourishes in the details. I loved taking out her festive dinner plates and using them for breakfast. *Yes, everyday is a holiday,* I said when Adele questioned why we are using the plates she had tucked away for special celebrations and holiday occasions.

By now she was in a wheelchair, her scleroderma, the immune system disturbance slowly moving into her organs. We did have fun. I loved indulging her whims. A new restaurant every night, although she rarely ate the entree, mostly waiting for the right moment to eat dessert. I remember taking her to an extravagant ice cream parlor in Dania Beach named Jaxson's saying: *let's eat dessert first*. A new concept for her, to break form and indulge. We rolled along the waterways, went to the mall; she adored watching the children playing at the designated child area at the Aventura mall. Her energy pulled away from being a critical judge to a more inward place of allowing life to be.

One night I heard a loud clap and went into her bedroom, the air was rarefied, and with a loud deep breath—her final—she exhaled. The air was filled with her spirit as I sat for many hours contemplating this holy moment that I was invited into—this passage of my mother, veils parted, doors opened as she slipped away. I went to the ocean that morning/mourning—to the mikvah of immersion. My mother died. Trusting existence, something deep happened, my mother was physically gone. I loved her, and we began a new relationship. Death took her body and love continued/continues. The beauty in the gift of life my mother offered continues. Sadness is when thinking stops. A sacred silence a new door opens, the door of the continuing beyond.

When I was 12 years of age I had a turtle, Myrtle, when she would hibernate it was through her slow shallow breathing that told me she was still alive. Yes, breath is life. Birth and death happening in each moment. This as a practice is a bridge, each breath rises and dissolves, especially true since we don't breathe in the future or past—a direct teaching—to be present now.

Adele remains alive in her hairbrush, a photo, her wedding song *Stardust* that she danced with Manuel my father: *And now the purple dusk of twilight time Steals across the meadows of my heart High up in the sky the little stars climb Always reminding me that we're apart You wander down the lane and far away Leaving me a song that will not die Love is now the stardust of yesterday The music of the years gone by. In my heart, it will remain My stardust melody The memory of love's refrain.*

Adele and Manuel Bromberg

Section Fourteen:
Bearing Witness: Finding Meaning

Memory is the initiation. Not to remember is equivalent to becoming the accomplice. Hence the vital necessity to bear witness. Not to transmit an experience is to betray it…To bear witness, yes writing is not a profession, it is a calling, an honor whereby we discover the perils and power of the word. Words can become spears, words can become rules, or words can become prayers and songs.
—Elie Wiesel

*A*ging brings me to heal the unimaginable, to discuss the unspeakable. Doors that had been sealed and hidden emerge to soften the harshness of calloused heartache. Iris, my sister, now with short term memory loss, for years there has been a seesaw tension between us, finally we are brought together into a familial tenderness. There are times when Iris divulges her unimaginable horror at having had a little sister—last night on the telephone she said: *mother was supposed to have a boy. Oh how I wished I could have pushed you back in. I tortured you,* or on my last birthday Iris called to say: *your birth was the worst day of my life.* Sometimes I cringe or ache for the small child who was greeted with such unrelenting anger and resentment from her big sister and wonder what happened to create the animosity and neediness that didn't allow Iris to open into love.

I remember singing a song together in a song booth called *Some Sunday Morning,* and in the middle of the recording I was pinched by Iris and started crying. I was 5 she 10. Now I smile and hold the memories and this child Paula more tenderly. Without an active memory Iris continues to remain my sister Iris, less chatty, more present to what is as she experiences less interests and the closing in of her life choices. Few outward adventures for she who lived in an entertainment realm. Movies, concerts, books, lectures, marketing, newspapers, phone calls, her home, errands, traveling, her car, the messy divorce with her husband Ronny the father of their three children, her deceased husband Bill who passed in their bed of a heart attack, her alcoholic middle daughter Heidi who committed suicide, her comfort of shopping; all in the past. And now the refrain: when all sisters and brothers will sing together—one voice as one heart—will be our Hallelujah!

She remembers me, I call with some regularity for a simple conversation, the pain arises and then I remember that loss was always present—she never liked me except as I aged and trained myself to be a good supply for her needs. Iris, the sister who never was! And now she is confused and fading in and out, diagnosed with short-term memory loss/ dementia/ Alzheimers; she appears to trust my openness to her dislocation, her disorientation, her disappointment and confusion. I have inherited a grandmother's heart, and am still growing to fill in the tenderness, to be humanized. To strengthen my character, to not turn away, to see with a generous eye.

The mystical power of memory. Without memory, our existence would be barren and opaque, like a prison cell into which no light penetrates; like a tomb which rejects the living. —Elie Wiesel

Each loss, every object that has come and gone has been a remarkable teacher deepening my ability, this capacity to love and cherish, to value this aliveness. The redemptive memory I carry is sitting in the back seat of our family car with my grandmother, my mother's mother, Mama, silently holding hands. Taking in the love and kindness of this beloved woman who spoke little, made homemade blintzes, lit Shabbos candles every Friday night with her head covered by a table napkin, bentching licht—blessing and lighting the candles, waving her wizened hands over the flame, my Mary Glassman, darkened from her years on the beaches of Narragansett Pier, Rhode Island and Miami Beach, Florida.

Mama was from Slonim, a town in the Grobno Region of Western Belarus, in Bialystock a city in Poland which changed hands repeatedly, shifting between Russia and Poland. In that time having a significant Jewish population that spoke Yiddish, historically spoken by Ashkenazi Jews. Colloquially, the language is called *mameloshn,* meaning *mother tongue.* Yiddish, a colorful deeply expressive language reflecting the color and flavor of a people who arrived in the Americas. It is older than the spoken English and considered to be the Robin Hood of languages.

Yiddish became the language through the mother, particularly because girls were denied an education, and carries the essence and soul of Jewish life. My home was flavorfully filled with Yiddish conversation since both Mama and my father's mother, Bubbe Zlata, only spoke Yiddish for the years that I was a child. Zlata was born in Malaryta a town in the Brest region of Belarus historically known as White Russia.

'Halevay, you should live hundred and twenty years, plus three months!' 'Thank you, But why plus three months?' 'I wouldn't want you to die suddenly.' —Yiddish saying, *Halevay* means a wish for you.

Mama, who was the oldest of three children, self-taught to read in Hebrew, English and Yiddish, became the reader in the upstairs orthodox religious services for the other women who had not been educated, not had the opportunity to learn to read Hebrew. My mother was proud to know this about her mother and proclaimed the story often to show my sister and I the value of discipline and how smart her mother was; even though uneducated she was self-taught. Eventually Mama learned English, while Bubbe Zlata who lived to be in her nineties remained connected to her Yiddish language.

Most of Zlata's children died during her lifetime. My father Manuel was her youngest and visited her often, although I don't recall him speaking with her in Yiddish as my mother did. Zlata remained true to her European Ashkenazi heritage speaking the mother language, Yiddish to her children and grandchildren, carrying prayer books as she traveled, remaining culturally Orthodox adhering to a strict code of modest dress—dresses that fall below the knees, arms covered to the elbows, high-cut necklines, a scarf, heavy thick shoes; everything in black—modesty was the essence and theme. I remember on weekends when I visited her home in Providence, Rhode Island Zlata would unscrew the refrigerator lightbulb, have pretorn toilet paper in the bathroom on Shabbos. We did not eat out as Zlata was strictly kosher. There was no TV and when we sat in the car she would hum and smile. A tall stately regal woman, self-contained and happy in her life.

Yiddish, the language which will ever bear witness to the violence and murder inflicted on us, bears the mark of our expulsions from land to land, the language which absorbed the wails of the fathers, the laments of the generations, the poison and bitterness of history, the language whose precious jewels are undried uncongealed Jewish tears. —I.L. Peretz

As I aged and connected to my heritage I was remiss to see that while other families taught, in fact embellished their native language, most Jews did not teach the language of their heart to the children; Spanish people speak Spanish to their children, Russians continue to speak Russian in their home, Polish families continue speaking Polish, Brazilians speak Portuguese—this has been a uniqueness of the Jewish people often based on the desire to be done with the extreme persecution and anti-semitism that pushed Jews to assimilate and not wanting the kind of recognition that comes with identifying a people to a homeland language.

Hebrew, as the official language of Israel, in my generation was taught to the male children and rarely to Jewish women, the mothers were not taught Hebrew continuing to speak Yiddish. Hebrew became Israel's national language. Most Israelis refused to speak Yiddish, it was a reminder of the Nazi regime, carrying a German flavor reminder of the holocaust of persecution.

I went to Sunday School and was taught the history and traditions of my ancestors, yet when my father died of a heart attack at the age of 53, I was 26 living in New York and flew to Rhode Island finding it deeply unsettling to not be included in the minyan, the communal prayer circle, simply because I am a woman. This made a strong impact and most likely sent me to other traditions for many years. Eventually I saw that until I embraced the heart of my own tradition there would be no base or foundation to build/dedicate my practice upon. I returned to study, to learn and with a not knowing mind to embrace, experience as disenfranchised; life is unfolding how do I want to live. To reinvent myself and stretch, to find the connection to my heritage and ancestors with compassionate generosity.

Born Jewish, a woman, grief for the missed moments, heartbreak for the rudeness, intolerance, judgements and hearts I thoughtlessly bumped against. What matters—this continuous practice that I know affects the universe, the sky, the seas, and all those I encounter. What we are so matters, how we live matters, and in this manner I have embraced the heart and melodies of a sacred tradition, the music and teachings, Shabbos, a time of renewed rest, the centerpiece, the queen with regal presence, peaceful and festive. To remember and sanctify, and the melodies continue to lift my heart.

*Do not be daunted by the enormity of the world's grief.
Do justly, now. Love mercy, now. Walk humbly, now.
You are not obligated to complete the work, but neither
are you free to abandon it. —Pirke Avot*

Section Fifteen:
Love Renewed

To live in this world, be able to do these three things: to love what is mortal; to hold it against your bones knowing your own life depends on it; and, when the time comes to let it go, to let it go. —Mary Oliver

Along standing love in this life, Odile, I have cleared the static and renewed the love that was a base for our time together. What did most of us know as love—drama, misunderstanding, not many tools to hold to cherish the differences—and we most always are attracted to difference, to contradiction. Without a bridge to love the differences we instead create war.

My affinity with the teachings and writings of Jean-Paul Sartre and Simone de Beauvoir and the sound of the French language transported me to Odile and onward to Paris. We strolled arm in arm along the River Seine, sat nonchalantly in French Cafes, had incredible ice cream at La Petite Ile, the little Island, lived in a historic building across from the french gardens, traveled to Montpelier, ate in quaint Parisian restaurants. We visited the Louvre home to the world's most iconic pieces and one of the oldest museums in the world, the Eiffel Tower, Montmartre's cobblestone streets, walked through the

Luxembourg gardens and the Parc des Buttes Chaumont, locally known as *the garden of love.*

Having lived for several years at a Fourth Way School, the Circle of Angels, a Metanoian Order with a Gurdjieff teacher, now, moving about in the world with a changed sense of being brought me to question, to look at how Gurdjieff created a School for the continuation of the practical work toward consciousness. How is it to live the teaching as a way of being? And what do I know of love, of being a beloved? All the preparation I had made for this great event called Love, and now, here I was a broken-hearted nobody not knowing the difference between blessings and curses. Dumbfounded, heartbroken, crashing into a wall of reality, Nothing to do but breathe. And all I had to offer myself was a broken heart.

Life is about engagement, a way of understanding, and this knowing has carried me through the years. I was graced to be offered direction and to have no answers, continuous questions and live into a reality of becoming a teacher hopefully here to awaken others to life as a teaching, life without answers, engaged and attentive to life as it is. With the possibility of living from a higher place of being. As I age I am able to resist surrounding influences, to not be caught in the current of life's distractions. To pay attention to this vehicle, this body.

I eventually traveled solo to Gurdjieffs' Institute for the Harmonious Development of Man at the Chateau Le Pierre at Fontainebleau-Avon where he created his

Fourth Way School. I was on a Gurdjieff search looking for the miraculous and the journey brought me to travel to the school he had created in 1943 during wartime and the Paris meetings held in his apartment until his death in 1949 with his students. Gurdjieff is buried at the cemetery at Avon, near Fountainbleau, near the chateau which had housed his Institute about forty miles from Paris. He stated that the inheritance he was leaving is the phrase: *Don't forget! Remember!*

Directing students to their inner work—not automatically, mindfully and with attention the Fourth Way work has set a powerful and continuing tone in my life. It was a teaching to become conscious of oneself, a universal teaching for deeper knowledge while remaining in life.

Ultimately the building became a nursing home and his School/Institute relocated to Paris guided by Gurdjieff's wife Jeanne de Salzmann and then their son Michel de Salzmann who I had meetings with, and through his suggestion eventually returned to New York. The offering was to live where a known language was established and to go deeper into the teachings rather than be caught up in a romantic dramatization that would not serve this awakening process.

Love is renewed, continues, form changes—and in the open space of no story a powerful shift happens beneath the surface. There was no longer Odile. Heart broken open I journeyed to New York. Everyday life, the teachings, filled with contradictions and disappointment, like a hammer swinging, nailing expectations. Are these distractions—used well these moments carve, cultivate depth. No goal and Paris the land of romance, City of Love, captures the inescapable reality of impermanence. All temporary, even the dramas.

Dew drips drips wanting to rinse away the dust of this world. —Matsuo Basho

Offering recognition and value to what has already existed, we meet ourselves in the fire of love. This is the gold, the treasures of aging—to clear away past hurts, heartbreak—to shift the deadly smallness and untie karmic knots. To cherish the tenderness that has splintered the heart. Space/time affords us the privilege of putting down anger, resentment, hurts, disappointment as we revisit our experiences and memories—not in sentiment—to transform and cherish that we live and made effort, had experiences, learned—to allow the grace that has been our life to fill and empty us, to imagine the unimaginable—that each pain and event was necessary and brought teachings to make us who we are today. The obstacles and hardships become our teachings, our blessings, our ships that carry us to a renewed day, to a new port.

Impermanence is the number-one inescapable, and essentially painful, fact of life. Everything vanishes. All conditioned things have the nature of vanishing. —the Buddha

Section Sixteen: Blessings

Every word has consequences. Every silence, too.
—Jean-Paul Sartre

Words—I have always loved/savored words. They design and hold my heart. Our speech is appreciation, instructing and guiding our narrative: *Bamidbar* translated as *in the wilderness, in the desert,* emerges from the root *to speak.* As the story goes, the people, the wandering people, lost the ability to narrate their own stories, which carried them into the slavehood of living other people's versions of who they were. Slave's to another person's version. Wandering for forty years in *the midbar,* the wilderness, both literally and metaphorically, the story continues, we discover our true story our ability to speak, our voice; and always a fresh and new narrative arrives. Blessings come from our ability to say our true name, our truth.

The privilege of a lifetime is to become who you truly are. But first—you must unlearn who they told you to be.
—Carl Gustav Jung

As I age and relook at my own narrative buried under *the look* of the other I see I am not those things I was named, assumed to be. Nor am I those things I was taught to avoid. I cherish aloneness, I adore space and quiet, gossip and chitchat are depleting, I love to study and learn, to reflect and consider, wonderful music, writing, meaningful work and projects, to be of service, dialogue, a beautiful intimate conversation, physical beauty, an aesthetic environment, integrity, tradition; on the other hand small talk, toxic family, sentimentality, gatherings, parties, having people in my home, appointments and schedules, colloquialisms, form without content; these are not the high flying characteristics that suit this person. And then I am none of this. All flavors, all colorations. All people get to be young, yet few have this great privilege to grow old, to age.

It takes courage to grow up and become who you really are. —E. E. Cummings

In conversation, talking about aging and life, the sage, my 97-year-old cousin Henry Bromberg, in another of his wisdom teachings, said to me: *to live like a smart gambler is to know when to hold them and when to fold them.* We had been in a dialogue regarding time and choice making. Henry sold his boat age 90 and his airplane age 92, and is no longer traveling to other cities and countries. Travel is only as useful as the stillness inside. Now he has inner travels and adventures. Yes the world is a beautiful place to be born into when we know and honor the timing of external adventures and travels, *knowing when to hold them and again the timing of when to fold them,* this is the banquet of our life, to taste and arrive to our satisfaction with life as it is. Our gratitude for the home and a beloved we have or don't have, the location we are in, the happiness that is in each moment regardless, the beautiful ark that safely carries us to the shore, to look at all things as a measure of grace. To be in the moment with our needs as we live into the wonder of this one beautiful world.

This morning the beautiful white heron was floating along above the water and then into the sky of this the one world we all belong to where everything sooner or later is a part of everything else which thought made me feel for a little while quite beautiful myself.
—Mary Oliver

Section Seventeen:
Work as Practice

Work is love made visible, and if you cannot work with love but only with distaste, it is better that you should leave your work and sit at the gate of the temple and take alms of those who work with joy. When you work you are a flute through whose heart the whispering of the hours turn to music. And to love life through labor is to be intimate with life's inmost secret, All work is empty save when there is love. It is to weave the cloth with threads drawn from your heart, even as if your beloved were to wear that cloth. It is to charge all things you fashion with a breath of your own spirit. —Kahlil Gibran

WORK IS LOVE MADE VISIBLE

To Be of Use

What is work and more so, what is our work? We teach this to our children. The enjoyment of life, the undifferentiated look at our tasks, our service that does not always ask financial reimbursement for time and effort. Living into the joy as we work, not as an obligation, a compulsion; work is a way to distribute the gifts of our love. And in life it can look like writing a book, making breakfast, emptying the garbage, choreographing a dance, smiling with a child, painting a wall, changing a light switch for a neighbor, washing dishes, sitting at a desk. The slight shift of emphasis from what we are doing to how we are doing it—to the love, the embodied compassion with which we are doing it—creates presence and radiance. Our acts are eternal gestures of love for all who choose to partake, and each opportunity is an inquiry. Life is a school, and the real work is happening deep down inside. What comes out is the true treasure, a perfect cup of tea served to a friend. Perform each task as if your life depends on it. It does!

After completing years of school why do we continue our education: called college. To forestall going into the world, or as many say to not go to a university we enter this world unprepared. Prepared for what. To be in a higher income bracket some would answer. Alan Lew, one of the most beautiful beings I have encountered, wrote: *This is real. This is very real. This is absolutely inescapable. And we are utterly unprepared. And we have nothing to offer but each other and our broken hearts. And that will be enough.*

I remember agreeing with my mother not to have a heart valve replaced at her age because of the high possibility that the surgery would advance her memory loss. I imagined I could prepare myself for my mother's death. Preparing how I would feel and deal with life without her alive. Impossible, to prepare for that—I experienced our indissoluble bond of love. Love made visible was the perfect action. I see now, to give it all away and then to know I held nothing back as we shared the final section of her life together. That was enough. The greatest preparation is to love.

Love will lay a carpet of treasures at your feet. —Rumi

Often, as I walk miles in the ocean I pause to talk and invariably I ask: what is your work? This appears to be the great ice breaker of conversation. The personal importance of accomplishment, of recognition, a title and identity as something/someone, the pursuit and ego that needs recognition, chasing money, being seen as important, security. There have also been moments when the person in the ocean meets me with an intimate conversation about a deeper understanding of what is work. This vulnerability, openness to engage in an exploration, to be seen and participate and cared about—a foray into possibilities and the unfamiliar, an invitation into the unknown, investigating as inquiry into what matters—sharing who we are as conversation. To love work for work's sake is a beautiful reflection. How to work, not as another doing preoccupation, but as a way of being.

Work is the place where the self meets the world. We stay alive and our work stays alive, through the willingness to remain the life-long apprentice. —David Whyte

In my years of listening to others I have come to understand that most people find comfort in some addiction, compulsion or fixation. Many gravitate to exercise, some to smoking, drinking, Facebook, thinking, digital equipment, food, drama, shopping, television, sex, travel, distractions, and the list continues. We all use something for comfort. Can we choose more prudently, wisely, how to uplift our addictions to promote harmony and health, service to this world? To move beyond the influences that are imprinted, our reactions have to slow down for particular qualities to find a place to see unselfconsciously. Reactions are automatic. Wherever we are and within each moment becomes our practice.

Writing and the beach are practices, years ago for me it was aimless and unnecessary movement; the recognition and decision to reframe my outward ventures allowed the beach and writing to settle my mind, focusing on what matters. The essentials—openness, clarity, integrity, alignment—my state. I have an acquaintance who reminds me that I often remark: *how is your state?* And she says she didn't quite know what I meant. Rather than hook into feelings like happy, sad, good, bad, anxiety, stress; a state lifts us to joy, wonder, ecstasy, love, gratitude—higher vibrational qualities.

The moment you have in your heart this extraordinary thing called love and feel the depth, the delight, the ecstasy of it, you will discover that for you the world is transformed. —Jiddu Krishnamurti

Love and work are inseparable, they are our two feet as we walk along a path of the heart. To forget one is to be disharmonious, out of balance; to embrace both opens us to the secret of life, the art of living. Work is a way to show up, to serve this world. Walking along the boadwalk, making dinner, serving a cup of tea, all are eternal gestures of love for any who choose to partake, and each opportunity is an inquiry. Life is a school, and the real work is happening deep down inside. What appears is the true treasure, a perfect cup of tea, beautiful food served to a friend, the guest. No conscious work is ever wasted. The only real satisfaction in life is to work not from compulsion but consciously. The work is to remember oneself.

The only work worth doing is to remember oneself.
—G.I. Gurdjieff

And what is my work? How to make conscious use of energy and bring inspired attention to the task at hand. Universities that are not teaching inner growth instead perpetuate solutions rather than preparing the soil for higher service. Self-importance, a preoccupation with the trivialities of one's personal life appear to stand in the way of deepening. How to become useful! Does our work have meaning and who makes that so. Does it mean more when I speak with a client than when I am writing, doing laundry or walking in the ocean? Am I of service with each moment? How to cultivate a steady reliable open heart?

Work is robust vulnerability. —David Whyte

From inner work we develop our ability to be of service. True inner work is timeless and formless. Attention and awareness have been considered to be the bedrock of every practice, and all of our work is a practice. What does it mean to live in awareness, to live in presence as love. Is that how we purchase products, is it truly a value we bow down to. Our culture has praised the success of wealth, even while we watch lives destroyed through fame, compulsion, attachment and addiction. I patiently watch my aging sister's mind slowly dissolve. Yes, she is more present than she ever was as a previously busy person endlessly engaged in entertainment and distraction. And then, is this presence? Certainly more simple as she chases a thought and then relinquishes any possibility of finding it. The world calls this sad, but is it?

The day you decide that you are more interested in being aware of your thoughts than you are in the thoughts themselves—that is the day you will find your way out. —Michael Singer

Into my eighties I no longer have the urge to travel or to outwardly entertain, distract myself. My availability to others remains, call me and I will pick up the phone although far less willing to listen to the minutiae of daily reporting chatter. Discovery, wonder, excitement; all the hallmarks of youth. How to retain that sense of delight, the passion for life. I go to the ocean, breathe, sit, be with the ever-changing ocean.

The main ingredient that I bring to work is to not be in the way. How to teach that? I don't know. How to step aside. In this life most professionals we go to we often indulge, distracted by the stories of the provider we visit. Their need to fill the air waves with and for their own personal entertainment is a common occurrence. Doctor, banker, accountant, acupuncturist, hair stylist. To hear about their children, their preoccupations, their daily doings. Can people step aside and show up? I consider this a genuine act of maturity, to drop the stories and show up. To be present to the what is. And within this lifetime to find a work we are dedicated to, to be willing to walk into the loneliness, the grief, the sadness, the happiness, the opportunity of discovering love, the willingness to open, to dig deeper, to discover worlds within worlds, to savor and digest our life, to be saturated and penetrated by our experiences, and to let go of the ground we have stood upon and to not know. Discomfort you are my dear friend. What then is our companion. Mine is the music. The spaciousness of the notes is where I rest.

At the still point of the turning world. Neither flesh nor fleshless; Neither from nor towards; at the still point, there the dance is, but neither arrest nor movement. And do not call it fixity. Where past and future are gathered. Neither movement from nor towards, Neither ascent nor decline. Except for the point, the still point, There would be no dance, and there is only the dance.
—T.S. Eliot

When I worked with autistic children, I directly entered their world, imitating and whirling together. I listened to children who had never spoken, finally speak. Such results confirmed my instinct to follow the child rather than follow the rules and guidelines. Our minds hesitate to tap into universal energy, we construct little worlds and boundaries and declare that to be the way, even though our energy could raise the frequency of the entire planet. To continue to live in the present moment is to be courageously willing to try new ways, not having to follow precedent, staying connected to the heart—to make love visible. In my work that is how I aim to live.

To Be of Use

*The people I love the best jump into work head first
without dallying in the shallows and swim off with sure
strokes almost out of sight. They seem to become natives
of that element, the black sleek heads of seals bouncing
like half-submerged balls. I love people who harness
themselves, an ox to a heavy cart, who pull like water
buffalo, with massive patience, who strain in the mud
and the muck to move things forward, who do what
has to be done, again and again. I want to be with
people who submerge in the task, who go into the fields
to harvest and work in a row and pass the bags along,
who are not parlor generals and field deserters but move
in a common rhythm when the food must come in or
the fire be put out. The work of the world is common
as mud. Botched, it smears the hands, crumbles to dust.
But the thing worth doing well done has a shape that
satisfies, clean and evident. Greek amphoras for wine or
oil, Hopi vases that held corn, are put in museums but
you know they were made to be used. The pitcher cries
for water to carry and a person for a work that is real.*
—Marge Piercy

Section Eighteen:
From Doing to Being

It is because artists do not practice, patrons do not patronize, crowds do not assemble to reverently worship the great work of Doing Nothing, that the world has lost its philosophy. —G.K. Chesterton

Action, camera: we are drowning in a world of activity and movement. Stopping appears to most as lethargy, laziness or depression. To unplug from external connections and reconnect to self is a deep transformative reset. Yes, this is a wondrous world of technological advancement, although so many caught in the doing are used by it rather than able to use it with balance and appreciation. Young people absorbed in the digital world, occupied by the random pop-ups on their phone, aging move into keeping up with stock market tickers and pressing *like* on other people's Facebook pages, shopping and other continuous doing activities without space energy for connecting to the still inner world that develops substance of being.

Simplifying one's life to extract its quintessence is the most rewarding of all the pursuits I have undertaken, wrote Matthieu Ricard, having been anointed as *the happiest man in the world* at close to 78 years of age through scientific studies that involved scans of his brain. Ricard, a French Buddhist monk, said: *if you instrumentalize the world for your own needs, see it as an instrument to pursue your own self-interests, it's not going to work. The goal is to bring happiness to others, to relieve suffering.*

This journey to emancipate from doing to being, a choice we decide as we relinquish the outer adventures for inner stillness: to ground ourselves in this age of activity and distraction is a tall order. The spiritual world—a familiar refrain has been *workshopping,* as people travel to workshops in the New Age world to acquire an identity, sometimes a new name in their search for meaning. Ashrams and finding a Guru became a story of the times. More currently, following the Covid epidemic, online master classes, visiting places through the digital media of zoom as constant companion, gathering impressions and information have continued; many find relief and enjoyment through the resources that were created for health and safety during the time of Covid.

These days I am confounded by the lack of books on the beach that are now replaced by boom boxes playing canned music to overlay as well as interrupt, displace the natural music of ocean, birds, shells, and wind. Digital reading on electronic equipment like iPhones and iPads have replaced the books we might remember holding in our hands. Rarely a hard cover book appears on a beach chair or blanket.

Ah, how good it is to be among people who are reading.
—Rainer Maria Rilke

To connect to the wonder in the natural world, the rhythms of the sacred mystery, that is the miraculous. Not to say there is an either/or—it's to know and nurture the soul-nourishing possibilities inherent in our organic world. Looking for happiness to oversimplify a complex world, using the stimulants of social talk-chatting, travel, shopping; a world of power, authority, right and wrong, a culture that has outposts in your head on how to dress, eat, and train the children. Our system is designed to promote and value ambition and financial wealth, rather than to see ourselves as a guest, amazingly alive, receiving what shows up, remembering humor, compassion and heart, creating an inner sanctuary as nourishment.

School throughout our formative years and then onward to college as the what to do, the structure of our culture is geared towards feeling less than for not attending college. A competitive world of athletes and concert musicians making exorbitant salaries, while teachers and service-oriented professions often struggle to pay expenses.

Let us discover the joy of celebration and magic in life, in our practices, our work, so that our life is not mechanized; for not hurrying is a higher priority—and our lives to become musical notes, as our song continues.

Not with a theme of worry, instead a music of spaciousness that connects us to larger worlds giving birth to ourselves.

We have a tendency to think in terms of doing and not in terms of being. We think that when we are not doing anything, we are wasting our time. But that is not true. Our time is first of all for us to be. To be what? To be alive, to be peaceful, to be joyful, to be loving. And that is what the world needs most. —Thich Nhat Hahn

Section Nineteen:
Art as Life

When we reach the top, keep climbing. —Zen proverb

Expanding the edges; when I lived in Santa Fe, New Mexico I remember the excitement and surprise walking along streets seeing sculpture and art work at the beginning and ends of roads, in the parks, on corners, at intersections. And I thought, *why not*? Who says we can only see art in a museum or gallery. The outdoor air around an art piece breathes life into its existence as it stands outside, uplifts the environment in its fullness.

Statues on the corner; when we stop we drop into the present moment, into a richness, our participation in the mystery of life. Not as a sleepwalker, to see the beauty of the roads and streets we walk on, in our environment, form and function, art with purpose—bringing the profound to the mundane. Streets and roadways that were built for function, enhanced and uplifted by the artist's eye. Carried further this ability to see the beautiful reframes how we walk through a world of surprises and amazement.

What we deemed plain, damaged, or worn out reveals its preciousness. It is in our love for what cannot be grasped that the real beauty of the world offers itself up in kaleidoscopic splendor. —Joyce Kornblatt

This mindset of openness, seeing new brings life to our years. As we age, how to live with a child's wonder and vision parenting with an artist's eye. The rigidity of cultural conditioning and the formitory apparatus of the mind lock this into place. Our desire and ability to shift perspective and practice opens the narrowness—a narrow path leads to self-absorption and self-importance, openness, leaving the comfort of the known—we are called to witness and partner, to be in relationship, this is our challenge. To walk in this world and be startled by her beauty; beautiful aliveness expands life when we pay attention.

Our attitudes are acquired, are personal, limiting and arbitrary. Studying what creates our attitudes loosens them expanding possibilities; meaning comes from our way of seeing, not from circumstance. How we see life changes the way life appears. Seeing life as a play with ourself as an actor, circumstances lose their power and we become unbothered by what happens. Training ourselves in this way we become more available to life as it is. Real change happens from the inside. Living from the center of life, seeing panoramas, this unbroken view in multi-direction, remaining vulnerable is living into the mystery; to witness and live reliably into a higher state.

Now in South Florida I step out onto the east balcony and see a gorgeous sunrise, panorama of colors as well as sunset hues from the west balcony. At times canoes row by eagerly racing a friend or a sailboat, a boat named *Monkey Business* or *You Can't Sea Me, Livin' the Dream;* people having fun on the intercoastal enjoying their small, medium, or large vessel.

To be intimate with the world is to ground into everyday activity. And the true measure of our life is in the daily moment-to-moment appreciation and artistry: life is the gymnasium of the spirit and we are the instrument, the medium, the force that receives and anchors awareness, to uplift the ordinary moments to their natural elegance.

To see beauty in an aging weathered face, a worn well carpet, a declining pet, aging hands, in shriveled flowers. Beauty is compassion for the broken, weary, fallen, hopeless. Through recognition we become the agents who bring out the inherent radiance, experiencing image and song playing within. Beauty: the frog kissed turning into a handsome prince freed of imprisonment through being loved.

It is a serious thing just to be alive on this fresh morning in the broken world. —Mary Oliver

Section Twenty:
Pandora's Box

To know and understand real change requires a long preparation and to want it very much for a very long time. A passing desire or a vague desire based on dissatisfaction with external conditions will not create a sufficient impulse. One's evolution depends on individual understanding of what one might get and what we must give for it. —P.D. Ouspensky

So many possibilities in our imagination. Having dreams of travel, I imagined going to Tahiti, onward to the luxurious beaches and live in a stilt house over the waters. I remember my friend Helen and I arriving at a private airport to hitch a ride with any pilot willing to take us on our adventure. That didn't happen. Timing is everything—and we dream—sometimes those imaginings take flight!

I did travel purposefully for many years, looking for the miraculous, meeting with wisdom teachers in countries where their teachings flourished. Germany, Spain, France, Puerto Rico, England, Belgium, Hawaii, Mexico, Israel, New Mexico, the United States—from Massachusetts across to California. Sufi Dervishes, Gurus, Ashrams, retreat centers, spiritual communities, Fourth Way

Gurdjieff Schools, many inspired and inspiring teachers. These were the adventures and journeys that brought me to the *Way of the Lover*, to be on the side of love, to consider each person from a heart of understanding. We are our understanding and out of that emerges what we want.

In retrospect, and that's one of the beautiful blessings of aging—the opportunity to understand, to recognize and see with awareness the deeper meaning of circumstances devoid of illusions as we look beneath the images to see the wonder of our own true nature. To give to humanity what we find within ourself opens the heart of the world. In this journey of self-discovery we come to know ourself through our interaction with life. We are midwives to a new awakening, the process itself is the gift.

And today a deep bow to all the teachers who have been a bridge, a link, doors and windows to consciousness. On a journey, an ascent up the mountain where I saw panoramas, vistas—and a very deep bow to the teachers who broke my heart. And the climb down the mountain to live in this world, in the heart, pierced, penetrated for our heart to shatter, uncompromised, cracking until one day breaking open. There is nothing more whole than a broken heart. The heart must break to become large, for the whole universe fits inside. To become that broken-hearted openness living at the center of love itself—it's in an open heart that the mystery appears, *when the beloved is born in the heart, the entire creation participates in the birth.* To pay attention to the present as the focal point of our life, it is all here and available to us to live in this everyday life. And the work is to be rooted, anchored within, to build love with a sense of aliveness that is right here originating from consciousness itself.

Those who have a 'why' to live, can bear with almost any 'how.' Everything can be taken from a person but one last thing: the last of the human freedoms—to choose one's attitude in any given set of circumstances, to choose one's own way. —Victor Frankl

I grew up in a busy household family where punishing and sadistic teasing humor were woven under a cloak of lovingness. The children were rarely sanctified or celebrated; no one attended my high school, college or graduate college ceremonies. And yet, to the outside world we appeared as a model, kind, loving, extraverted community-oriented popular family—my mother was the president of most of her activities. Head of the parent-teacher association, president of the women freemason group, Hope Link, president of the temple and her Crestwood Country golf club.

Image, cliches, money and blaming were everything and this life value continues with my sister, Iris and her children today. My father traveled for business and made an effort to placate and keep peace in our home until he would erupt in anger at the impossibility of the task at hand. He was certainly *Mr. Nice Guy* asking for little and hoping to be asked for little in return, generating the illusion of calm diplomacy. I was the anomaly.

Take the stones people throw at you and build something beautiful, use them to build a monument. —Ratan Tata

The family worked hard to put me in dresses and stockings and pretty shoes—to this day no make-up, wearing shorts and a hoodie, sneakers, a naturalist beach where I serve as a beach ambassador, writing and studying, teaching, practicing; a psychologist/teacher working with many communities throughout the country. To do something because we understand rather than because we are told makes for a tremendous difference. To react is easy, to understand comes through mindful awareness, through getting out of our way—there are not many understandings there is only one.

Dysfunctional families cater to the most toxic person. The other family members do everything in their power to keep the toxic person happy. Everyone walks on eggshells and the mood in the house is dependent on the toxic person's mood. —Laura K. Connell

I remember when I applied to the New School For Social Research and chose philosophy as the major my mother was appalled. *What do you want to be a philosopher, there's no money or future in that,* said Adele, my mother. I more often then not called all family members by their proper names. Mother was Adele, father, Manuel or Manny, sister, Iris. Stripped of their titles in my mind—these were individuals to make peace inside myself, and the reality was to see things as they were.

If you want to have a happy day, stop arguing with the way things are. —Adyashanti

My sister Iris' consistent constant put-down, insults were: *why do you have to analyze and try to understand things?* Manny's continual laments were: *just make your mother happy,* Adele's sister Anita and their mother, my grandmother Mary—who I called Mama, pleaded: *don't upset your mother.* The world turned on keeping Adele satisfied, and I seemed to be the thorn in that balloon. Continuously. And as heritage this was passed on to Iris, her world turned on everyone in her family keeping Iris happy and out of hysterics, creating dramas with her alcoholic middle daughter, Heidi, who committed suicide, and her self-absorbed drama-oriented son Mitchell and her eldest indignant self-righteous daughter Vicki, who continued this plagued heritage with her son, Jacob, who she chose to medicate rather than live with his passionate excitement towards life—the biblical *sins of the father are laid upon the children* continues. The iniquity of one generation passed on to the next. The idea of ancestral sin, or the passing of sins from one generation to the next is a central theme in the Bible—which also says that remembering/awareness to the sins of our parents might assist us to show up differently to our own lives and to future generations.

Iris married an immature self-absorbed young man, Ronald a Navy Ensign who sexualized their middle child Heidi, and youngest son Mitchell. Iris and Ronny placed Mitchell into a mental hospital for observation since the insurance company would only pay if he was hospitalized. Mitchell imagined that his mother, Iris was poison and he was their puppy since Ronny preferred his dog to his children, so Mitchell ate his food on a plate placed on the floor under the radiator. I adored baby Mitchell and lavished him with compassionate tenderness, although that provoked envious Iris to one day say: *I will make certain my children never talk with you, you are not their mother and I must always come first to them.* Ronny demanded that I don't visit their home fearing that I would infect them with my bohemian lifestyle. What an ironic narrative, the projections and fears carried in people's minds. I did ask Ronny not to bring his girlfriends to my home, in respect for my sister. Yes, roots grow in bitter soil: before we sweeten the fruits to become agents of justice and love we need time, dedication and a willingness to go down into the darkness where the roots drop into the earth. Strength comes from solid deep roots in the ground.

Families: where abuse and neglect are permitted; it's the talking about it that is forbidden. —Marcia Sirota

How to get off the blame train so as to live anew

rather than continue our inherited story. So often when I work with people they arrive with the story of their perfect happy childhood, until we look closer. Pandoras Box—don't open it unless willing to release/dismantle the myths and tales of your imagination. And yet. The box also contains hope and a treasure house of fine jewels—a journey away from ego and materialism towards virtue, wisdom and the freedom of aliveness.

Family disfunction is like fire in the woods that rolls generation to generation taking everything in its path until one person has the courage to face the flame.
—Terry Real

I gravitated to a work that promotes awareness and self-understanding, the key being understanding. The starting point is always uncritical self-observation, a verification through our own experiences to arrive at a place of self-awareness. Choosing awakening as our purpose we learn to use this ordinary life with its daily happenings, its uncertainty, suffering, pleasures, to come into a real life.

Awakening is possible only for those who seek it and want it, for those who are ready to struggle with themselves and work on themselves for a long time and very persistently in order to attain it. —George Gurdjieff

To liberate the stories we no longer can insist on being right. How to live in uncertainty, in broken heartedness, to stir up the bottom and sit in the sea of fire. We are invited in to help put out the fires—to choose hope. This is our challenge. To be the blessing and to see the blessings. Hooray for this privilege to uplift and eventually drop all the stories.

Pandora was cautioned not to look within herself. Opening the 'lid' to her inner being would have irreversible consequences difficult to bear. For most of us, Pandora's box—which represents the great mystery of our inner shadow—remains unopened. Why are we so afraid of facing ourselves? —Dr. Mariana Caplan

The situations and circumstances of our life are binding or freeing. They are not arbitrary nor are the conditions necessarily limiting. These exercises can be used well like hurdles when we are no longer fascinated and instead willing to see the theme and bigger picture of life. No longer trapped by the events we can well use them as a path to our awakening. With humor and grace we step up and out of the well onto dry land. Paying homage to what brought us this far, lifetimes; we sanctify our history, our birthright and inheritance, our heritage and lineage—shattering the cage we heal ourselves in the fire of understanding, then we have the possibility of a conscious life.

Wear gratitude like a cloak, and it will feed every corner of your life. —Rumi

Section Twenty-One:
On Love

To love is first of all to accept yourself as you actually are. 'Knowing thyself' is the first practice of love. May I learn to look at myself with eyes of understanding and love.
—Thich Nhat Hahn

When I traveled with Adnan Sarhan, Sufi master, drummer and inspired belly dance teacher, his invigorated precision brought fire to both dancers and meditators through the power of his drumming. We traveled to numerous countries together and his message was simple: *Live in the present before it passes you by and becomes past.* Pay attention to the real needs of the moment, this became theme in those years that I journeyed with Adnan.

The path of love is like a bridge of hair across a chasm of fire. —Gregory of Nisa

I wanted to be a drummer and create a tempo and aliveness in myself, in listeners, for the dancers. And so I drummed and understood that it was my own aliveness, the love that communicated through the drum—the stamina and passion that penetrates to unite body and soul from the fire of our breath. How we strike the drum is as important as what we drum.

Loving is the greatest freedom and fulfillment, so the wise, being wise, cash in on that. —Rumi

Eventually I was living in the Sufi Community, ignited through the drumming and whirling, a dervish practice of turning. Ancient sacred chants, dhikr/remembrance, rhythmic repetition of devotional attributes, meditative movements all practices to develop the higher intelligence of the heart.

Nestled in the Manzano mountains in Torreon, New Mexico was the Sufi Foundation of America retreat center, with Adnan of the Shittari order, a master of non-intrusiveness, creating a system of spiritual practices seated in breath, movement, chant, prayer, fasting, turning, belly dance and drum. Drumming creates a vibration for belly dance, an embodied spiritual practice connecting the dancer to the earth, to live into the moment, a surrender to the dance empowers. And the music—heart beats alongside drum beats, song of the turn, swaying arms mirroring the flute, singing in this choir of love.

Hey, that was joy that just stopped in for a visit! Glad it came by, I was wondering where the hell it had been. —Rumi

Love is a direct route; once we step-aside, are burnt away, only love remains. The heart broken open until the entire universe is placed in the heart. Closing our eyes we open the eyes of the heart to become the heartbeat of the beloved.

The practices and living in New Mexico, the land of enchantment accelerated the momentum—big open sky, tent, hammock, wooden table with a Swedish outdoor cookstove, huge vegetable garden, wide horizons; life simple, minus the accoutrements: Hallelujah!

The rose opens because it has heard something. The cypress grows strong and straight because a love-secret is being whispered. Elegance in language arrives in response. Love with no object, conversation with no subject, seeing with no image. Light on light, pure possibility. —Coleman Barks

Traveling

Living in more than five different spiritual communities throughout the years—Sufi with Reshad Feild, Mevlevi with Shaikh Kabir Helminski, Sufi Foundation of America with Adnan Sarhan, The Circle of Angels Metanoian Order with Gurdjieff Fourth Way teacher Jean Robertson, Hindu with Mata Amritanandamayi and Jewish Renewal.

Listening to stories from the students who had also lived there, I wondered what Gurdjieff, what Fourth

95

Way School, which Rajneesh, what Sufi Mevlevi and dervish community they had lived with, since it rarely reflected the one where I had lived, even when they were there at the same time.

I recognized that the climate of the environment impacts the level of being of each person. How they are impacted continues to refine the original nature they had when they join the community. I recognized that to live at an ashram, an intentional community, a spiritual school as a mature soul or as a banana you don't leave as an old soul or as a grapefruit. Who you are in essence remains your nature, that doesn't change: having experiences creates an experienced mature soul, yet one remains the person you were when you entered: what can shift is the level of being, the refinement; maturity and inner integrity are the bridge. Maturity is the flowering—to live in the present moment with awareness, our personal transformation, to let our heart be broken open into wonder, the magnificence and privilege of this life. How to live an ethical life, to develop a moral integrity that embraces all of humanity, is this love being crafted at any community?

And so we meet along the way people who have traveled, lived in community, in ashrams, participated in numerous teachings and retreats while keeping their ego intact never quite tackling the underlying psychology that creates distress and suffering for themselves and others. Spiritual teachings without grounding in psychological work, without unraveling and digesting our history and family system, leads to vanity, bondage, corruption, delusion and illusions. This invitation to not pretend—to be handed the mirror—a clean cut through illusion, no fanfare, the whole drama collapses when no one shows up to play the lead. This is the beginning of the real, in the smile, in the silence.

How can we cultivate the openness to say, there's more for me to listen to, more for me to explore, while also pausing and saying, thank you. —Rabbi David Ingber

The same is true for the nuclear families we grow up in. Embellished stories of fun holidays with tinges of sentimentality fill the air waves of memories devoid of looking underneath at the sacrifices and giving-ups that were required to create, to sustain the illusions. This observation, has been a teaching I have employed throughout the years that I taught groups at Esalen in California, at Ghost Ranch in Abiquiu, New Mexico with Dr. Elisabeth Kubler-Ross as well as in New York City. What is heard may not be the original intent, like the children's game of telephone to pass along what we hear. It changes as we repeat and pass it along, as well as how we digest and experience information.

I don't know how people have used our teaching conversations through the phone lines—once the conversation stops it's up to the other to use or not. My work has been availability, deep listening, being witness, to show up and be of service, to ease the suffering and dispel or shift the narratives, the incomplete unfinished ongoing stories.

There is a language older by far and deeper than words. It is the language of bodies, of bodies on bodies, wind on snow, rain on trees wave on stone. It is the language of dreams, gesture, symbol, memory. We have forgotten the language. We do not even remember it exists.
—Derrick Jensen

Circumstances and the events that happen to us are not the root of our suffering, how we relate to those experiences is what creates suffering. The blindfold off, barriers dissolve. Regardless to the storms that appear, or how rocky our days seem to be, there is something greater that embraces us, so in each moment while our nature may or may not alter the circumstances our receptivity to what is births consciousness. When we experience separation rather than openness, when smaller emotions lose sight of the bigger picture during a storm, leading into doubt, it is our ability to step back; to witness through understanding we transform our life.

Jeanne de Salzmann spoke wisely when she said: *In order to see, we must first learn to see; this is the first initiation into self-knowledge. First of all, we have to know what we must look at. When we know, we must make efforts, keep our attention, look constantly with persistence. Only through maintaining our attention and not forgetting to look, one day, perhaps, we will be able to see. If we see one time we can see a second time, and if that continues we will no longer be able not to see. This is the state to be looked for; it is the aim of our observation; it is from there that the true wish will be born, the irresistible wish to become: from cold we shall become warm, vibrant; we shall be touched by our reality.*

Our attitudes are acquired, are personal—the odd mixture of caring and unkindness, our dysfunctional early home conditions and our culture do not nurture the growth of an authentic human being. We are taught from family to believe we are being loved: a threatening difficult concept to sit with—we might have been cared for, yet, love and emotional abuse, insults and put-downs can not coexist.

Our lack of understanding and confusion about the meaning of love; we don't have to love—we choose and learn to love and the lack of definition adds to the mystery of those of us who didn't truly feel loved and are therefore unable to love. And so our literature and news reports are filled with the destructive result of so-called love. Homicide, suicide. Divorce, stalking, rape, Bluebeard and domestic violence, La Belle Dame Sans Merci, the frog prince, Rapunzel and Cinderella: all about so-called love.

I love you, said the man. *Strange that I feel none the better for it,* said the woman. *Until you have wisdom and power equal to your love, be ashamed my sons and daughters, to avow that you are in love. Or, since you cannot conceal it, love humbly and study to be wise and strong. Aim to be worthy to be in love. Conscious, developed love is the wish that the object should arrive at its own native perfection, regardless to the consequences to the lover or family. Conscious love begets conscious love. It is rare among humans because, in the first place, the vast majority are children who look to be loved but not to love; secondly, because perfection is seldom conceived as the proper end of human love—though it alone distinguishes adult human from infantile and animal love; thirdly, because humans do not know, even if they wish, what is good for those they love; and fourth, because it never occurs by chance, but must be the subject of resolve, effort, self-conscious choice. As there are works of art, so must conscious love be a work of art. Such a lover enrolls himself, goes through his apprenticeship, and perhaps one day attains to mastery, He/she perfects his/herself in order to purely wish and aid the perfection of his/her beloved and/or family.* —A.R. Orage

Our work: to soften the heart, to open, not turn away, to humanize this world having the courage to bless each day, alive in fullness infusing the planet with our awareness.

The modern nuclear family has become a pressure cooker in which the parents' problems with love and intimacy are passed on directly to their children. How each of us expresses and receives love in relationships—and fears doing so—was established long ago, in our very first intimate relationships—with our mothers and fathers. Our parents have a tremendous influence over us, not just because our well-being depended so totally on them, but because they were the first people we loved deeply. Unfortunately, our first loves usually leave us with wounds that we carry with us for the rest of our lives.
—John Welwood

Once we envision and taste the extraordinary, the challenge and practice for us as custodians of this planet is to build a new world. We are placed here to learn how to love. A worthy investigation for this lifetime.

This is love: to fly toward a secret sky, to cause a hundred veils to fall each moment. First, to let go of life. In the end, to take a step without feet; to regard this world as invisible, and to disregard what appears to be the self. Heart, I said, what a gift it has been to enter this circle of lovers, to see beyond seeing itself, to reach and feel within the breast. When you keep your heart open through everything, your pain becomes your greatest ally in your life's search for love and wisdom. —Rumi

Section Twenty-Two:
Theatre

At Emerson College, in Boston, Massachusetts, I studied theatre and aspired to be a drama critic inspired by the Boston based dean of American theatre critics, Elliot Norton. His precise crisp analyses made significant contributions to the development of theatre criticism in our country, a true visionary defending the artistic freedom of writers. His willingness to engage artists as well as to evaluate and encourage their work earned Norton a respect that few critics receive. I was motivated knowing and training with Norton, and had fun writing reviews for local newspapers in Boston, Massachusetts.

My philosophical bent brought me to study Greek theatre; the roots and substance of our culture in theatre—our western theatre is rooted in ancient Greek amphitheater, open-air theater in the round and mythology. And so I went to the theatre writing reviews, loved analyzing the various aspects of each production—acting, lighting, audience response, raw overall execution, choice and levels of meaning of the script—a great vocation for this theatre lover. Yes, theatre was an important influence to my life, and continued through my study and training in psychodrama rooted in Greek drama.

I studied and trained with Dr. Jacob Moreno at the Beacon Institute, a psychiatrist who pioneered and collaborated with his wife Zerka. They understood spontaneity, how creativity propelled human progress forward; psychodrama with impromptu dramatization used roleplaying for investigative, insightful self-presentation. Often positioned on a stage, open-design circular arrangement, echoing ancient tiered and interactive group dynamics, psychodramas were conducted at the Moreno Institute, Beacon, New York and I invited my parents to attend, to observe as I played out a personal psychodrama assisted by Zerka where we mutually explored phantom limb theory. Zerka had her right arm and shoulder amputated age thirty-nine due to a chondrosarcoma and I with an enucleation of the right eye from a traumatic eye injury age two and a half with a protheses at age seven. A phantom limb is the sensation, the perception of discomfort that the amputated part is still attached possibly due to the brain's attempt to rearrange sensory signals.

The mind in action was Zerka's explanation of psychodrama, *Don't tell me, show me*. And showing to Zerka meant acting it out. Psychodrama makes the invisible world visible. Because there is no script we interact on the spur of the moment, here and now.

My mother lived in a world of creating proper images to mask delving deeper, not to risk offending others. Appearances, self-deception—unsettling childhood memories became rearranged, sometimes forgotten, sacrificing depth to maintain an image of admiration and achievement, disabling access to an interior world until the mask becomes the face. To Adele being in emotional pain equates to being a loser. The deceit is in fashioning the image; deformities and aging are hard to tolerate and for Adele and continuing with my sister Iris their self-pity victimization and martyrdom, feeling trapped by circumstances was an arm-twister used to manipulate others. Sympathy and self-pity were their blind alley. I was the thorn puncturing illusions to show up investigating, exploring the what is, witnessing our personal family trauma to create meaning and value. Ironic! My relationship with my mother contained humor and drama; I pushed boundaries and there were many surprises, adventures and love.

The philosopher Wittgenstein said: *To learn about the self, step outside of the self.* The humanity of the other person we are portraying, the one we are often in conflict about, enables us to see and perceive in a different way. This improvisational drama is a way to live, is an attempt to find ourselves in a new way and recreate, rewrite our life. I loved working within this genre, finding resonance, self-reflection and understanding through reenactment. Particularly effective with children to open a door of imagination and see beyond their own position, to begin to sensitize to other roles: father, friend, sibling, mother, teacher, caretaker; to not be limited by our personal position is a seed for compassionate loving-kindness.

I continued this rich work when Jacob and Zerka Moreno opened a center in Manhattan. Psycho-drama, literally a drama of the mind and soul, and there in New York City at Moreno's Institute we reenacted scenes from our lives in our effort to express unexpressed memories and practice new and more satisfying behaviors, gaining insights. In this approach I was exploring ways that theatre and drama can be used for therapeutic purposes. To take on varying roles and explore different perspectives is a powerful tool for personal growth and self-discovery.

I continued to teach psychodrama at GROW Institute in Chelsea, New York City, eventually meeting Fritz and Laura Perls who developed the thread of psychodrama into Gestalt Therapy. *Awareness in itself is healing,* said Fritz Perls, his approach designed to show up, to create greater awareness of the experience of being in the world. Rather than looking to change ourselves the focus is to develop awareness, be present processing things in the here and now. Laura Perls was my supervisor and I trained to become a Gestalt therapist at their apartment in New York City. My work with her focused on integrating the past into the present and as we sat with other practitioners I marveled at Laura's ease and creativity. Her manner of supervising resonated with how I am, less focus on the clients I was meeting and more on the connection to those in the group and how I experienced myself with each client. I trust this approach and continue to use myself as the test and measure, like a camera lens resonating to what is on the screen. This was the entranceway to embrace conversation as a modality of being and teaching.

My education continued at the New School for Social Research in New York City, through an interactive relationship, dialogue with the professors. American existential psychologist Rollo May, American poet Alan Ginsberg, social critic Paul Goodman, African-American poet laureate Leroi Jones. Author and professor, my friend Edith Kern.

I was inspired to be an interviewer. And so I interviewed Holocaust survivor, author and Nobel peace prize laureate, beloved professor, champion for human rights and dignity, Elie Wiesel, Sufi Shaikh and translator of Rumi, Kabir Helminski and English mystic, author and spiritual teacher, Reshad Feild. The exchange of energy through those conversations—honest open dialogue fosters authenticity. Intimate conversations with a spirit of inquiry creates a new uplifted world as we meet our life freed of illusion and sentiment. Relationships in this way serve as a mirror to see and hear ourselves. Satsang, sohbet, wisdom surfaces. When we meet, seeing the reflection we enter heightened awareness setting a new paradigm, a discipline of the heart.

The word theatre comes from the Greeks. It means the seeing place. It is the place people come to see the truth about life. And the social situation. The theatre is a spiritual and social x-ray of its time. The theatre was created to tell people the truth about life and the social situation. —Stella Adler

The struggle of your life is your paradise, said Eido-roshi, and this mantra led me to be in life as it is. Revolutionary and revealing, unfolding layers and garments of acquired habits and impressions. How to get to the frontier of presence with integrity and wholeheartedness is the quest. Opening, being in our heart, holding the integrity of our values, heightens our energy. Shakespeare understood the theatrical nature of human existence: *all the world's a stage, and all the men and women merely players: they have exits and entrances, and in time we play many parts.*

Theatre is an art form of the present. It exists only in the present, and then it's gone. —Simon McBurney

Section Twenty-Three:
My Mentor: Bonnie Whittingham

I was brought to Bonnie by a friend Gracia Berry. Bonnie at the age of forty-four lived in her art studio on Cape Cod, Massachusetts. I was twenty years old and teaching at a Waldorf School in Greenwich Village, New York. And that began a long journey with my mentor, Bonnie Whittingham who inspired an apprenticeship that navigated this life for the next many years. Like Alice in Wonderland and discovering that adulthood arrives with its own freedoms, Bonnie was a paragon of creativity and imagination, a force to reckon with. We became Tweedle Dee and Tweedle Dum, the low and high instruments—I, a violin, Bonnie clearly a drum; as well as the Queen of Hearts: *off with her head.* Bonnie danced to her own drumbeat and in my tutorial I was brought to live out of the margins, to follow my own inclinations and ask for what I knew to be in my heart.

Bonnie had been a student at the Barnes Foundation and was told she would have a substantial financial prize and grant if she altered the size of her painting to fit the specifications of the awarding jury. She passed up the prize, in the hope of changing the rules of the contest for the freedom of creativity for future students. I adored her integrity and values, her close adherence to respect for her work, the truth of this life, and her dedicated practice to color and form. Bonnie was a pioneer in the art world of color palette; she ground her own paint: her oil paintings breathed richness.

She studied Rembrandt, the great masters, spending years developing her signature work of harlequins and masks that represented life and death. We named her studio in New York the Masque gallery and she became artist-in-residence there painting portraits and wonderful canvasses as well as sculpture and watercolors.

We lived together in an apartment on Thirteenth Street, Greenwich Village, New York. Bonnie had a small long and narrow studio where she painted masterpieces. Neither of us had much income, I was a student at the New School for Social Research while teaching at the Little Village Waldorf School. I walked around in the day to find Masonite pieces and canvasses that people threw away to bring home. Bonnie would gesso the panels to cover as well as build up the foundation before painting over what was there. Sometimes when she sold a canvas we would go to Neti's, a wonderful art supply store in the east village and carry the large, stretched canvas through the street to our home—linen if we hit a gold mine. Over the years we moved into two huge duplex lofts on Twentieth Street in Chelsea, New York, where the spaciousness invited Bonnie to create large, beautiful canvasses lightening her palette and adding the medium of sculpture, carving in stone, engraving and etching. We created a uniquely imaginative loft, one season when we left for Cape Cod we rented our home to Jane Fonda and Donald Sutherland. Such were our ordinary adventures.

On the Cape we had two connected cottages across from the Provincetown Playhouse on the edge of the beach near the center of town. Bonnie painted gorgeous rugs on the wooden floor, and locals would come by to view the *art on the floor*. She exhibited at the Art Association and various galleries throughout the country, eventually to be inducted into permanent museum collections and large corporate buildings. We were a joyful foursome, Bonnie and her beloved dog, Iggy, me with my bicycle and Weimaraner, Seal, walking the beaches and dirt roads of Cape Cod.

Bonnie's practice of happily painting every day brought me to wish to someday have a creative practice that fueled my day and life. The fruition of this dream realized itself in writing. Grateful to have a writing practice, it's the service I offer to myself, how I digest my life, and the revision/editing is to let the fire show through the smoke. I read and read my words again and again, as Bonnie painted all day and then would turn her canvas upside down and paint again. How I adored watching her work progress in its cycles—her courage to allow the painting to unfold—to live in the unknown, to dedicate her life to this art.

A bird doesn't sing because it has an answer; it sings because it has a song. —Maya Angelou

And so I write. My dear Elie Wiesel said: *not to transmit an experience is to betray it; this is what tradition teaches us.* And so I write. This sacred holy blessing—to discover the words, in my home, amongst my books, this house of study and teachings, this home with her altars and candles and Bonnie's paintings. The books might be banned, could be burned and still the letters, the words rise. Last night I read pages of this book to my sister Iris who is in a memory care unit in Boston, Massachusetts, and she responded: *each word is a blessing to my memory.* This week, on my birthday, a canvas of Bonnies was at an auction and I bought it and put in up in my bedroom yesterday, yes, life continues, arrives when we pay attention.

When I wanted to go to the New School for Social Research in New York City Bonnie took me to the Dean and sat in the outer office as I went in to explain that I wished to attend the college and needed financial backing. My parents did not approve of the background of the schools progressive intellectuals who began the institution as a more relevant model of education. The founders took a public stand against U.S. entry into a war, the first world war, to create a new model of education for adults, a school where we could learn and exchange ideas with scholars and artists representing a wide range of intellectual, aesthetic and political orientation. Perfect for iconoclastic me with a strong desire to learn and for my abstract random mind-set which did not resonate with my earlier three years at Emerson College in Boston, Massachusetts.

The dean at the New School told me I could have a scholarship to cover all costs, although earning no matriculation degree. Learning would be for my own inner journey and not for achievement. Easily agreed upon and onward to study, to absorb a world and an ethos of challenging academia, asking big questions about the world. A school that dared to be different; dialogue with brilliant creative minds like Allen Ginsberg, Leroi Jones, Rollo May, Paul Goodman, John Cage, James Baldwin, Hannah Arendt, wisdom teachings from the artists, writers, philosophers and theorists who were creating and changing the world. They were human beings writing testimonies to their lives. I was drawn to the presence of individuals who created a relationship with their students, teaching from inner dialogue, creatively cultivating intelligence, originality and initiative. I saw that it wasn't only the ideas that were engaging me. It was the availability and exchange, the presence, energy, interest, co-operation and human interaction, the vitality and creativity that entered the classrooms and created the background for teaching. True education has a spirit of inquiry that creates a new uplifted world.

Years passed and the Dean called me into his office to commend my earnest dedication and devoted study and practice and offered to matriculate me, and I graduated and continued at the Graduate Faculty of the New School. Bonnie's impact mentored me in this lifetime for these adventures in wonderland, her unique vision of a world whose boundaries are as infinite as imagination itself.

There is a place like no place on earth. A land full of wonder, mystery, and danger. Some say, to survive it, you need to be as mad as a hatter. Which, luckily I am.
—Alice In Wonderland

Painting by Bonnie Whittingham

Section Twenty-Four:
Conversation

Conversation is a source of nourishment. Nourishing and healing communication is the food of our relationships. Many of us suffer because our communication with other people is difficult. There needs to be mindfulness and skillfulness on the part of both the speaker and the listener.
—Thich Nhat Hahn

When I lived in Santa Fe, New Mexico, I wanted to host a radio show and a friend of mine, Alan Hutner, producer of Transitions Radio, suggested we call it *Shrink Wrap* a double entendre regarding my work as a therapist euphemistically called a shrink, and the huge art world in Santa Fe where tourists came to buy art and have it framed or shrink wrapped in cellophane so they might carry it home on the plane or in their car when traveling.

The show didn't materialize and moved me onward to the next adventure in South Florida when A.J. Farshchian, M.D. stem cell physician, specialty regenerative medicine invited me to sit in a weekly position as psychologist consultant for his television show *MyMedicineTV, the Arthritis Show*, eventually to include hosting my own TV show-series *Conversations with Dr. Paula* interviews with professional people in the medical/healing world. In conversation with doctors of varying specialties, a chef at a vegan spa, yoga and pilates teacher, a radiologist and other creative professionals I invited to dialogue and interview. The work fit me, the art of conversation meaningful exchange, creative teaching conversations as a practice.

Deep listening is the kind of listening that can help relieve the suffering of another person. —Thich Nhat Hahn

It has been said that when we speak we teach, when we dialogue we clarify, when we listen we learn. A good conversation strengthens who we are. We become familiar with what is important. True conversation empowers, changes lives. To engage in a conversation, not talk or idle chatter, deepens us. It is a process, an experiment involving risk, an adventure where we agree to belong to the conversation. Practice and study like every art makes our words sing, have real meaning, can bring us to a new part of ourselves. This is conversation as a practice, the ingredients are presence, being active as well as receptive, asking a real question. Mindful inquiry, moving away from colloquialisms, pat expressions, generalizations, allowing for space, and, ultimately, our being sincerely authentic.

I have continuously had a work I dedicated my life to, larger than I imagined as the conversations reaches into whole families, impacting children and their communities through a witnessing presence, gathering experiences from the private and personal to the public and universal. Yes, work is love made visible; living from the center of life demands clear intention. Seeing the sacred in all things is the ordinary practice. The circumstances of our daily life serve as a reminder, are the invitation.

We have been given a mind, we have to know it. We have been given higher mind, we have to earn it, to find it. We have been given receptivity, we have to develop it.
—William Segal

I remember deciding that an important teaching for the community that invited me to teach a weekend retreat would be how to have a meaningful conversation. I accepted the invitation to teach at a vegan retreat knowing that to sit together, to have meals with each other throughout the course of the week we would have to learn how to engage in conversation. Children learn through imitation yet they rarely see adults engaged in deep dialogue, they aren't taught how to create the mutual vulnerability that's required to engage in true conversation. What followed our lively class was the proof of the experiment—when we gathered for dinner at the round table sitting outside together—thirteen members of the class—this was quite different from most dinner table conversations. People listened, available and open, space was offered to digest the previous comments, there were silent moments, as well as depthful interaction, listening, not turning away, slowing down, purposeful, belonging to the conversation—savoring, digesting both the words and the food—what a wonderful week-end.

Good conversation is energizing. To listen to the gaps in between the words—is no longer speaking from the circumference. Mindless chatter is an energy leak that sabotages truth. Developing skillful conversation starts with a willingness to emerge a slightly different person and involves risk. It makes sense and elevates our life to have mindful conversations rather than absent-minded distracted words reporting our day's events, telling what other people are doing, empty phrases with a lack of accountability. Our conversations in the spirit of inquiry informs our life with meaning. Speech is the mirror of the soul, we are what we say. And from this place I continued and continue to develop my life's work.

When you speak, allow the insight of our collective humanity to speak through you. Our communication is our continuation. It's what we put out into the world and what remains after we have left. In this way, our communication is our karma. —Thich Nhat Hahn

Section Twenty-Five:
Rabbi

Ultimately, our questions must emerge not from mental categories but from deep within the heart. They must rise to the surface of our beings as we sit in silence, so that they are not just the old questions which we raise whenever we have nothing else to talk about or just for the sake of argument. They need to be the questions which will make a difference in our lives. —Reb Zalman Schachter-Shalomi

Living in Santa Fe, New Mexico, connected to reform Temple Beth Shalom, meeting innovative spiritual teachers such as Reb Zalman Schachter-Shalomi, one of the originators of the Renewal movement and ecumenical dialogue, as well as my remembrance of what brought immense healing to my soul, I wanted to be a rabbi. The chanting prayers and melodies, the encouragement to embrace, to renew a healthy spirituality within Jewish life spoke to my heart with the hope and possibility to repair myself and the brokenness in the world.

The ancient Talmudic saying is: *Whoever saves a single life is considered to have saved the world.* The sanctity of life promotes resilience, courage, integrity, responsibility and acts of kindness. This gathering of light ignites my spirit. I studied and participated in a rabbinic program for those years, took on the project of creating a local Jewish cemetery and a Chevra Kadisha, a holy society—a group of volunteers who see to it that the bodies of deceased Jews are watched/guarded, cleansed from death to burial.

Our goal: to live life in radical amazement, to get up in the morning and look at the world in a way that takes nothing for granted. Everything is phenomenal; everything is incredible; never treat life casually. To be spiritual is to be amazed. —Rabbi Abraham Joshua Heschel

When my mother died we said blessings placing a tallit/ a prayer shawl, around her shoulders, the one that had been a covering, a canopy or *chuppah* under which we stood during our marriage ceremony at Temple Beth Shalom in Santa Fe, New Mexico symbolizing a sheltering holy presence and the blessings of a new home we hoped to create. I have continued a deep connection to the roots of my heritage as well as a heart alliance to the teachings of sacred awakened divine beings.

The higher we climb the deeper we must bow.
—Reb David Ingber

As I studied I understood holding a space for liturgical music, maintaining traditions—Shabbos, lighting candles, saying kaddish, yizkor, memorial prayers, yahrzeit the anniversary, the remembrances that maintain connection and reminds me to not be idle, to hold to the difficult, to the continuation of life. The teachings pass through me—are me, and as a classmate reminded me at her rabbinical ordination *you already are that.*

Rabbi from the Hebrew rav means teacher, and most responsibilities—leading services, performing a wedding or burial do not require an ordained person to perform life cycle events. And so, as I studied completing a par-arabbinic program focused on ritual leadership and community service; invited to officiate life cycles I created sacred wedding services, offered counseling, officiated at baby naming and funeral services as a response to the needs of community. Liturgical tunes in my head bring solace and wonder, renewal and uplifting.

Wisdom-teachings from most traditions speak to the necessity and truth of direct experience as well as to the ability to transform, integrate and live in a manner that sparks of holiness imbue our daily practices. The Zohar, a foundational work of Kabbalistic literature, says: *You beings on earth who are in deep slumber, awaken! Who among you has labored to turn darkness into light and bitterness into sweetness? Stop sleeping! Wake up! What are you waiting for?*

The spiritual practice of the tradition gave rise to Jewish Renewal, brought soul and deepened the spiritual connection to an ancient tradition, where we become partners with existence, opening the heart of prayer and song and how we live our inner life, opening gates of awareness to the interconnectedness of all of life.

Tradition continues to teach, and we are included in the partnership looking to renew and receive the treasures of our ancestors.

The study and inner practices of a tradition direct us to awaken the heart of kindness. The Hebrew word Rabbi means teacher, and a spiritual connection reflects that understanding and wisdom are guided by a higher power. This interactive posture to align ourselves with higher forces, called *spiritual intimacy* by Reb Zalman: the range is the entire cosmos, the upper paradise.

The love we experience is nurtured through a system whose range is the entire cosmos and a life task that serves to order life in harmony with this, no other consultation room is so laden with significance.
—Reb Zalman Schachter-Shalomi

Section Twenty-Six:
Adele

I went hunting, looking for the mother inside, we went reaching out for the mother inside. Birth and death in every breath, tears for all souls merging, I went singing for the mother inside. —Miten

My birth mother, Adele Rosalind Glassman Bromberg Hellman, had many faces. She chose Rosalind as a middle name after seeing the opera *Die Fledermaus* where Adele was Rosalinde's maid. A socially active person, and for many years I regarded her as a cross between Ethel Merman and Lucille Ball, two characters she really liked. There was often a drama to Adele's life which she drew on for energy and story. I moved to Florida to take care of her, and that eventually was an ending story, the finale.

I remember my mother having had many medical issues, an autoimmune disorder that expressed itself in Raynaud's syndrome, systemic Scleroderma and undiagnosed celiac disease. During her life time these disorders were not commonly known about and gluten-free as well as healthy eating were not in mainstream information. Juice bars and residential community golf courses were popular in Florida and my mother spent her winters in

Fort Lauderdale as she aged. Health food supermarkets did not have the popularity they now have. And while she indulged in the doctor circuit she did not participate in the prescription drug system. Her activity focused more on the energy from conversing and entertaining the doctors albeit they lacked knowledge and information about the causes of her physical maladies. I remember when I took her to the chief cardiologist at Broward Hospital in Fort Lauderdale, Florida, and declining medication he commented: *come back when you turn blue. Oy,* said I.

We all have a theme that drives our life, we can ignore or cover it, distract ourselves or manage it with many different postures, regardless, it does has energy and influence in our life. Adele lived in a family that ridiculed and diminished her medical plight, actually they called her a hypochondriac and rolled their eyes when she talked about visiting doctors to treat her flare-ups.

Life circumstances became the finger-pointing towards each medical situation, and so the death of her brother Willy at the end of the war: the story is told that he was in a small boat in Japan April 2, 1945 readying to come home when gunfire from Japanese snipers killed him. Harry Glassman, her father, age 56, reading the telegram about his son as he sat in his car parked in their driveway on Bellevue Avenue in Providence, Rhode Island collapsed slumped over the wheel and died of a heart attack. Adele's first born, Iris Ruby, was colicky and had difficulty keeping food down. The next pregnancy, a son, died at birth, and not too many years later, age two-and-a half, a wire from a stuffed toy bunny penetrated my eye and required her challenged decision for eye surgery or possible blindness.

If the Beloved said: pay homage to everything that has helped you enter my arms. There would not be one experience of my life, not one thought, not one feeling, not any act, I would not bow to. —Rumi

This was Adele's narrative and blame for her auto-immune disorders and her nervousness—how we frame our life, our viewpoint is how we read our life, a larger perspective brings us out of a narrow subjective world so that our personal suffering might be looked at as the suffering that connects us to a larger world. For her each circumstance was a direct hit personally aimed towards her and not useable as grist for the mill, rather reinforcing a victimhood encouraging self-pity and the martyrdom of misfortune. Her arm-twister was to cleverly manipulate others, sometimes suggesting someone or something stands in her path of happiness; an unmarried child, their physical condition, or even the whole medical system. The pleasure of sympathy is a blind alley since it doesn't create change. Feeling trapped by circumstances and helpless to lift out of this viewpoint, the fantasy of being right feeds the hypocrisy.

Adele and subsequently my sister Iris have both garnered admiration, attention and approval from family, friends and most people around them, holding much of their family hostage in support of their position. Both at times displayed a face of prolonged suffering, like wearing a crown of thorns while being thrown to the lions. Iris speaks nonstop of her daughter Heidi's death, never mentioning suicide, and Adele spent years barraging her immune system; Iris and Adele provoked guilt, neither accepted/owned any responsibility for their attitude or behavior.

Birth order theory claims that the first-born is aligned to the father and the second child is positioned with the mother. That certainly was demonstrated in our home and in Iris with her second born Heidi. My sister Iris was more connected to our father Manny and at the dinner table sat next to him while I sat next to Adele. I felt protective towards Adele as Heidi did to Iris, and when we were with other family members if they were competitive or unkind to my mother I felt irritated and distanced by their innuendos or their glances that often went unnoticed. This was passed on through my sister Iris who later in life just didn't like Adele or me. These alliances get perpetuated and create division in so many families. We read the biblical stories of Joseph who was his father's most beloved child—his brothers eventually threw him down a well selling him into slavery, Cain who murdered his brother Abel, the prodigal son, a parable, provides us with lessons about family rivalry.

We are conditioned by our family constellations and

unless addressed they imprint our choice making and how we see the world. Nurture or nature was my question and apparently both play a large part to who we are and how we show up in the world. Without understanding we are as spiritual teacher Gurdjieff said *food for the moon.* As I see it we are used up by our circumstances, locked into a life where we have little ability if any to create our own meaning. Our automatic and reactive thoughts, emotions and behaviors eat up our energy and continue to do so until we make our life our own. When we react it is a mechanical reaction without thought or understanding and when we respond there is someone present who is intentional, decides whether to be angry or not regardless to the circumstance. It is very possible through practice, understanding and maturity to be more than a automatic reactive machine, to become conscious, living in an intentional manner.

The self-fulfilling prophecy draws in the adversity that has festered in the resentments, the you owe me, imagining being rewarded for birthing and raising a child and ultimately draws in the adversity both Adele and Iris have drawn through complaining and blaming and disappointment as misfortune in their minds finds a way to their door. Painful experiences could be transformed into valuable and meaningful understandings.

Without a hurt the heart is hollow. —The Fantasticks

I saw my mother as a character and laughed, some-times cringed, at many of the situations she created for herself. I remember going to meet her at the international airport in New York, watching as she was wheeled off the plane. I raced onto the platform to see what happened. She said shhhhush and whispered in my ear that she had pretended to collapse so she wouldn't have to declare the fur coat she was wearing that she bought in from one of the countries she visited and so the airlines ordered a wheelchair and brought her off the plane before anyone else debarked and therefore didn't bring her through customs. I considered her escapades like that of an Auntie Mame. Yes, often life was a theatrical play with Adele being the central character.

Mother ocean, mother earth, mother nature, mother sun: I was named Ambika Ma Devi by Amma, in Sanskrit the name given to me is the mother of the universe and all beings, an original energy force. Adele was indignant, displeased that I would refer to Amma as mother. *She is not your real mother, she never changed your diaper or was awakened in the middle of the night.* I smiled at her literalness and reaction, understanding the difference. Amma was a spiritual mother, a representation of mother goddess, a source of life and fertility. Devotee of the divine mother, a mahatma meaning great-souled, honorific title of love and respect. Mata Amritanandamayi Ma Devi is known as Amma or the mother, spreading selfless love and compassion towards all beings. This idea, ungraspable by Adele; a step into an expanded universe where global intimacy becomes a possibility. To embrace our birth mother as she is and be reverent and respectful is to drop into the dharma, the cosmic law that upholds universal natural laws—a combination of morality and spiritual discipline that has guided my life.

How do we use this life rather than be used by it. Could be one of the questions that moved me to become a family therapist, a psychologist/teacher motivated to listen, since listening is the great art of loving. And then more—to repair through softening the heart, to go beyond the resentments and armoring—to open the heart, to change the narrative: for there to be reconciliation and forgiveness—to be available to the grace that is always raining and to choose connection over isolation. The broken places are cracks to let the light in.

Be like a lion outside but like a flower within. Let us strive to reach a state in which we are able to see all beings on earth as part of our own Self. —Amma, the mother of bliss

Section Twenty-Seven: Ocean

I am in love with Ocean lifting her thousands of white hats in the chop of the storm, or lying smooth and blue, the loveliest bed in the world. In the personal life, there is always grief more than enough, a heart-load for each of us on the dusty road. I suppose there is a reason for this, so I will be patient, acquiescent. But I will live nowhere except here, by Ocean, trusting equally in all the blast and welcome of her sorrowless, salt self. —Mary Oliver

I wanted to be a beach bum and travel the world to pristine island beaches. And so many Island beaches I visited, oceans I swam in, until this present moment where my full length east windows overlook the Atlantic ocean as the desk where I write faces the south east section of ocean that beckons my heart. Large horizon over the ocean, clouds form and roll hues of blue that penetrate as sunlight passes through the atmosphere scattered by air molecules that disperse all colors of light. The sea acts like a sunlight filter light spectrum. Praises to this eye that can see, this ear that hears, a heart that flows, this aliveness I am.

I chose to train and serve Haulover, a clothing optional naturalist public beach near my home in South

Florida. Clean sand, often crystal clear water and well-trained available lifeguards. Having access to this beach has elevated and brought days of joy, comfort and a small community of committed beach-goers to my life. I wrote portions of my last two books at the beach, sometimes I read, write, bring lunch, set up an umbrella and chaise lounge as well as a small chair, quietly sit alone, walk miles in the ocean, drink lots of water and am in heaven. Simple and exceedingly grateful to listen to the sounds of ocean and wind and to breath in oxygen released from the sea; this meditation soothes my soul.

The sea casts her spell holding me in her net forever.
—Jacques Cousteau

My childhood summers were spent at Narragansett Pier, Rhode Island, a picturesque beach town. Our family rented a house, I loved the beach life. Age twelve hurricane Carol made landfall with winds over 120 miles, storm surge and powerful winds caused ocean water to rise and flood most of the area. My father Manuel and sister Iris were working at Benny's office in Providence, a New England retail chain of thirty-one stores founded in 1924 by my uncle Benjamin Bromberg, and as my mother and I made our way to our green Chevy parked in front of the house a tree fell on the car making our getaway impossible. The ocean water rolled up the street covering the open lot near our house, filling the roads. Phone lines down, we embedded ourselves in the house,

I was twelve, not one to worry or fret, this was a big adventure and an experience of the unpredictability and magnificence of mother ocean. I was hooked. And here I live and write, finding the inner stillness amongst the background of the sea that rhythmically comes and goes.

Your heart is the size of the ocean. Go find yourself in its hidden depths. —Rumi

Section Twenty-Eight:
Intimacy

Intimacy is the art and practice of living from the inside out. Intimacy is related to our sense of having been wounded, and the startling intuition that my way forward into life, or into another person's life will be through the very doorway of the wound itself. Intimacy invites me to learn to trust the way being wounded has actually made me more available, more compassionate and possibly more intimate with the world by being opened in ways I never realized it was possible. —David Whyte

I wanted to have a mutual love with one person, each of us loving the other at the same moment. I had experienced yearning and disappointment in relationships, unrequited love, sentimentality, bickering, blaming, criticism as well as passion, attraction, kindness and creative alignment. How to surrender to the differences and be in mutual vulnerability, intimacy. So many partnerships are rooted in compromise and misunderstanding rather than enthusiastic appreciation, gratitude and the unfolding of uncertainties. How beautiful to have love received and reciprocated. To know that one of us might continue, will be available even as our beloved disappears. To bear this is a risk of loving, taking great courage to enter the maelstrom, the whirling stream, the current of life.

What more could one ask of a companion? To be forever new and yet forever steady. To be strange and familiar all at once, with enough change to quicken my mind, enough steadiness to give sanctuary to my heart. The books on my shelf never asked to come together, and they would not trust or want to listen to one another; but each is a piece of stained glass whole without which I couldn't make sense to myself, or to the world outside. —Pico Iyer

Who is the soul-mate we magnetize, this other who is our own true self. I am blessed to have earned and dedicated my heart longing to a beautiful beloved. Mutuality—we live together, loving and caring, vulnerable and beholden. Stretching to our differences, knowing that the lack of toleration for differences creates war in this churning confused young soul world. Old souls know love is the atmosphere, vibration, frequency that resonates with an open heart. Unlimited, boundless eternal, intimate. I have often imagined that the source of healing this world begins with embracing the differences of the other.

The only way to heal the world is to heal yourself first.
—Dr. Elisabeth Kubler-Ross

The practice of loving another human being has brought me to my knees, humbled and opened as I develop and deepen throughout the years. This journey into loving-kindness, mutuality has stretched me to face

133

my shadow, to compromise and celebrate the miracle of life as it is.

If we have nothing but each other we have so much.
—Andrea Gibson

And the teachings continue as we walk together, sleep side by side, eat meals, listen and practice gratitude. How lucky a shared lifetime of softening the heart, of leaning into each other.

The world is not comprehensible, yet it is embraceable: through the embracing of one of its beings.
—Martin Buber

Section Twenty-Nine: Writer

I have always imagined that Paradise will be a kind of library. —Jorge Luis Borges

I wanted to write non-fiction books. An avid reader, this cherished source of warm friendship began early in life, a way to remove my mind from emotional upheaval and drama, rather to sit strongly digesting my life. At the age of thirteen I was reading Jean-Paul Sartre's *Being and Nothingness,* a philosophical masterpiece that delved into questions of existence, consciousness and the nature of freedom.

Reading *Cell block 2455 Death Row* by Caryl Chessman, a condemned man's words, his memoir strongly impacted how I looked at the world, investigating the issues of personal conscience, integrity, responsibility and the challenging necessity to remove oneself from the world, even to be incarcerated for the karmic experience of placing oneself in a situation of surrender to re-evaluate life. Chessman lived on San Quentin prison death row twelve years, escaping the electric chair seven times. His case propelled a movement to abolish capital punishment in California.

The third book directed me to enter into a relationship with the other, asking questions I carried on how to be open while creating alliances with medical people, how to nurture myself and participate with a medical community. *The Plague and I* by Betty MacDonald who contracted tuberculosis in 1938, also known as consumption and the white plague, once a large part of this culture, it was common and often deadly until the disease was lessened by the advent of antibiotics. MacDonald was forced to enter a sanitarium with little social contact. Using wry wit and keen observation she translated her difficult life experience writing books using humor and vivid storytelling. How to look at a serious subject with an honest fresh viewpoint—her memoir; using her experience as a teaching she humanized the possibility of transforming a challenging medical condition into an engaging narrative.

I spent my summer school vacation time in Boston at the Mass General hospital in a unit where most of the patients were eye trauma military personnel, men airlifted with head wounds mostly blast fragments metal shrapnel embedded in the eye from combat conditions. Connecting, experiencing the wholeness of each patient I encountered created a bridge, a ladder from the wound to be on the side of love, with the collective courage as sanctuary, childhood became that Biblical question: *where are you? How are you?* I was a little girl rolling around the hospital in a wheelchair to visit, touch hearts to others in our similar situation.

The disfigured created ambiguities, bewilderment, until I became a stranger to myself and silent; disappointment covered the absence of what was missing. How to be seen as a whole person rather than what the medical world saw as an injured part. As a child those questions rose in my heart in my effort to humanize both the patients and the doctors. We are here to learn together, each walking our own path—to become more human, to live with kindness whatever our profession. And this faith I have carried in humanity, this hope for a response to each other—to listen, to pay attention, yes, there are many ways to serve and with sincerity we might find our moral compass. Greeting another human being is a step into faith, into being human, a practice; we are all guests carrying our brokenness, mending, restoring so we aren't strangers to ourselves or to each other.

With wounded faith, I wore a locket that had a blindfolded woman at the head of a ship. One day my teacher Jean said now you have a faith that sees, a faith that continues to walk with questions, not answers. One Hasidic teacher said, *No heart is as whole as a broken heart.* Elie Wiesel added: *No faith is as whole as a wounded faith.*

In the introduction of my earlier book *The Way of the Lover, a Way of Understanding* titled *An Invitation: To Remember Yourself,* I reflect that the approach towards self-knowledge that has served me has been to perceive my life as pieces of a puzzle. One day one piece fits, the next day another, eventually creating a recognizable harmonious pattern. To begin to see the configuration, although not necessarily while assembling it. As the pieces cohere I didn't have the overall concept, the bigger picture, since I was in it—living my life—until the *Aha*.

Sometimes it happens early on; the privilege, another of the benefits of living into a long life, into the eighties and then some, is that we might have that *Aha* at some point. In our inner inquiry we have moments of clarity and access to the greater picture. Those flashes of truth allow the brief intervals. Story drops away, we have glimpses, we wake from the dream able now to remember and live into a consciousness called reality. Faith is the pilgrimage, trust is the destiny, I am learning to sanctify life, to give thanks to everything that has brought me to this moment.

We each have our own story of the life we think that we are living. But underneath this story lies the deeper truth of who we are—our real nature—and a life that is fully present. —Llewellyn Vaughan-Lee

Entering the mind of articulate people who process their life drew me to Jean-Paul Sartre and his lifelong companion, Simone de Beauvoir. Love is a partnership and according to de Beauvoir, *if you love someone you love them as an independent whole.* Their relationship propelled me to look for a mutuality and what she named *authentic reciprocal appreciation of each other.* The meeting of two equal and independent minds. It's recognizing that the other is their own person. I studied the partnership—even to travel to Paris and sit in the cafes they had inhabited to feel their energy. Sartre emphasized choice and the inherent vulnerability of relationship, love as a constant act of creation, and recognizing and respecting the other's freedom. Sartre and de Beauvoir were a couple for more than fifty years, he claimed her to be the love of his life, ultimately to both be buried in the same area in a Parisian cemetery. They had remained intellectual and romantic partners.

One's life has value so long as one attributes value to the life of others, by means of love, friendship, indignation, compassion. —Simone de Beauvoir

Those three books marked steps of life questions that intrigued me: relationships, conscience, integrity, life purpose, the connection to being in a body, and to see others as community, a spiritual comradeship.

Reading at the kitchen table, and in later years on subways, I often carried a book, a friend to have with me under most circumstances. I loved words, alive with richness, as I also appreciated a good conversation, not chatting or explanatory description, or gossip—I valued heart-to-heart connection, honesty, reciprocity, meaningful dialogue. Reading and writing opened doors, tore down walls—asking questions, not expecting answers; the current of life was a surprise and I adored the connections and valued understanding as a way of integrating, opening the door to come home to who we truly are. Still do! To recognize and understand deepens our being, to understand reveals interior connections. Writing became a practice of self-connection, and as I age, self-discovery and revelation.

A writer's job is to give the reader a larger vision of the world. Writing is the act of discovery. Know that you will eventually have to leave everything behind. The writing will demand it of you. Writers are great lovers. They fall in love with other writers. That's how they learn to write. They take on a writer, read everything by him or her, read it over again until they understand how the writer moves, pauses and sees. That's what being a lover is: stepping out of yourself, stepping into someone else's skin. As writers we live life twice, like a cow that eats its food once, and then regurgitates it to chew and digest it again. We have a second chance at biting into our experience and examining it. —Natalie Goldberg

Writing with Natalie in New Mexico many years ago I saw her love for innumerable authors and was encouraged to allow my nature and attraction to specific writers flourish. Here, in South Florida I continue this joyful practice reading all the books of specific writers: Norman Fischer, Pico Iyer, Elie Wiesel, Natalie Goldberg, Joan Halifax, Thich Nhat Hahn, David Whyte, Alan Lew, Andrew Harvey, Delphine Horvilleur, Daniel Ladinsky. I have become one of the rarities here, reading a hardcover book on the beach, I smile and oftentimes approach whomever is reading a *real* book as I do my beach walk and pass by someone holding a book. The small meaningful things of life we fondly esteem.

We write to lure and enchant and console others, we write to serenade our lovers. We write to taste life twice, in the moment, and in retrospection. We write, like Proust, to render all of it eternal, and to persuade ourselves that it is eternal. We write to be able to transcend our life, to reach beyond it. We write to teach ourselves to speak with others to record the journey into the labyrinth. —Anais Nin

Section Thirty:
This Ageless Aging Body

And I said to my body, softly, 'I want to be your friend'
It took a long breath and replied, 'I've been waiting my
whole life for this.' —Nayyirah Waheed

I wanted to not be overweight. My younger less sophisticated illusion was: *if I lost weight that would be the end of all issues and problems.* So not who I am in a deeper understanding and yet we live in a culture that feeds us this malarkey. Yikes! Now for many years I walk with a healthy weight, not overweight, looking *normal and average sized*—life still throws curve balls. Discovering there are no winning techniques to navigate through life, there is only awareness.

Living into the moment life offers the teaching. Our culture is based on assessing who appears attractive, who looks young. Whatever is in your life be that, practice, not to complain—complaining is thinking—a willingness to live current, open, *lu yehi,* let it be, this is our great possibility, our true wealth. Explanations, justifications, rationalizations take us away from the heart and place us in a cycle of spinning thoughts.

The very center of your heart is where life begins.
The most beautiful place on earth. —Rumi

Moderate pain keeps us here and here is now. The core of our practice is the open experience of what is, without anything else interfering. Not about fat or thin. Certainly we have thoughts, impressions, attitudes: allowing the body to navigate and direct makes for a good dance.

Low level pain in my head has brought me to pay attention to being present. Why to mask the pain, or to disregard this messenger of awareness. Aging I also have been gifted with a new discomfort underneath the phantom eye pain, trigeminal neuralgia arrived. Two points of attention, practices to remember myself. To smile at life's treasures on this road of awakening. And so when I see others masking their pain with drugs, alcohol, marijuana, sugar; with compassionate understanding I hold their difficulty suggesting they use well this calling card of attention. Something will be our practice and rarely is it more than we can handle. Life's rhythm brings us reminders that are useable when we adapt to the value of what pain brings. The body speaks.

If you bring forth what is within you, what you bring
forth will save you. The body never lies. —Marion Rosen

There is an element and a very strong piece of me that believes pain is a microphone. My pain does me no good unless I transform it into something that is good. Chronic pain, still I continue to dance and sing, this can be done.
—Lady Gaga

The most awakened yoga teacher I have practiced with is Mathew Sanford, paralyzed from the chest down, confined to a wheelchair, his teachings: what it means to live in a body, inspires a true message of what it is to live in an ageless body as a whole person. These miraculous bodies that house mind and spirit.

Originally I taught myself to leave my body and float through the ethers. A kind of meditation that allowed me to see beyond the walls. A profound skill of surviving painful trauma until, rushing through life, speeding along I walked into a Ryder truck side mirror which smashed into my head moving my nose to the side of my face. And met my teacher Jean who touted that it took a truck hitting me in the head to bring me to a teacher. A lucky lifetime, indeed.

I was also blessed to study with Meir Schneider, born blind, self-healed to see once again. Living into the reality of how magical our bodies really are when we listen, when we practice self-healing. I know that we have to practice something in this lifetime, why not begin with a practice of self-love, self-caring, strengthening the mind to direct, uplift and have fun in this lifetime.

Hope is the dream of a waking man. —Aristotle

To bring attention, to be rooted in the ageless body—is to love and honor physical form as an expression of our infinite soul. Ageless is the joy of existence. Satisfied and complete with how we are. Over the years we might diminish interest in the drama and noise. This state of not knowing is the ticket—life arrives. To become honest, deepening our integrity, our practice matures. This is the privilege and advantage of aging. To learn to see who is beneath the rhetoric, opinions, thoughts, imprinting—clarity—like watching a movie named *this is your life,* without juggling to make alterations or self-judgment.

99 percent of people born between 1936 and 1946 (globally) are now deceased. Alive we become one of the rare one-percenters. And so, as many of the concerns fade away, sometimes they expand from our personal concern to a life understanding. What is the meal of life, especially since we all eat. What do we choose to nourish our mind, what activities, how we include food and exercise all have impact on this vehicle we name as body. And when the inside matches the outside we begin to live harmoniously, as connected, integrated wholeness.

To allow the natural radiance of aging in an ageist patriarchal world attuned to altering; to cultural patronizing. Within a systemic practice of oppression, inequity, we unmask our tenderized truth regardless. Aging or ageless, hair whitened, face lined, each line a mark of love as well as sorrow. Character displays herself on the face, each line carved in the face-mountain. Adversity and hardship reveals hidden strengths and beauty. The Western marketing slogan for aging well, the commercialization of youthful characteristics have led to a rise in injections, hair coloring, skin care that tout no lines a mirage to reshape and sell fashion, trends that make a business of youthful appearance, yet not manifesting stronger internal life-force.

Should you shield the canyons from the windstorms, you would never see the true beauty of their carvings. People are like stained-glass windows. They sparkle and shine when the sun is out, yet when the darkness sets in, their true beauty is revealed only if there is a light from within.
—Elisabeth Kubler-Ross

We walk through this life within a body, this miracle, our human physical vehicle carries us from birth to death, our special acquaintance we live in and with. The more intimate we become with our body finding safety and feeling trust we come to learn how our body generates energy. Listen to her, this friend of friends. She speaks to us through her energy and our love connects us to a friend who loves us free of judgment, and who has been with us from the very beginning.

Humor, playfulness, knowing the language of our body, listening to her requests and deepening our relationship, less reliant on outside opinions, turning toward ourself as loyal companion, the loneliness and isolation diminish as we develop a relationship with the companionship, with the garment we wear throughout our life: the clothing of our soul.

Talk to her, listen, pay attention lovingly and she will provide; service to the altar, the living sanctuary/refuge we enlist as we dwell in the midst of this incredible world. Loving your body, she has her own wisdom, she knows how to dance, this instrument, this beautiful mechanism whether we are physically asleep or awake she continues to serve us.

To be grateful is to quiet the mind that creates judgments and restrictions. Through every season the art of living is our preparation to live in gratitude as we are, in step in rhythm with life. When young, be young, when old, be old; not a renunciation of life, a transformation into a great adventure.

In your heart a flame is burning; your body is a light around the flame. —Bhagwan Shree Rajneesh

This very body the buddha, a treasured gift, the instrument that grounds and roots us. A bridge between you and the body. The body has immense wisdom and oftentimes doesn't need me to continue and maintain life: she breathes, dances, moves, vibrates, performs an array of functions automatically: heartbeat, digestion, internal temperature regulation, adjusting blood pressure, salivation, among other processes. Watching the body as she moves, sits, eats, is a preclude to observing thoughts, feelings, moods; all to deepen our observer, this eternal process of self-transformation. Watch your body, this miraculous friend. And eventually there is grace and surprising beauty as to how our body moves throughout the day. Pay attention: watchfulness hones consciousness.

The body is the vehicle of the soul, a vehicle of cosmic energy. We are not just bones and blood and flesh, we are magnificent conduits of energy that make us laugh and dance and live. —Chris Griscom

Section Thirty-One:
Gifting Our Smile: True Conversation

I wanted a work that inspires dedication, remembering Gibran's words: *all work is empty save when there is love.* The work we do, not necessarily relevant to its form, is who we are when we are authentically ourselves. My Gurdjieff Fourth Way teacher, Jean, had offered me an exercise to change the form of my work with clients who worked with me in my position as a psychologist; to loosen my identification and separate from a title that creates distinction.

This exercise brought me to travel to Native American pueblos, trading the gold jewelry I owned for turquoise jewelry to eventually sell during my travels to European flea markets with my Sufi teacher, Adnan. Continuing this exercise, I purchased used vintage Hawaiian shirts as I traveled through Hawaii with Sufi students to sell at flea markets when I lived on a ranch in Tucson, Arizona, and continuing when I lived in Santa Fe, New Mexico, at the Tesuque Pueblo Flea Market on Native American land. The numerous booths at the market displayed artisan pieces: textiles, woven baskets, ethnic beads, intricate carvings, brightly patterned bags along with rocks and minerals.

I designed my booth with amethyst geodes which are round rocks that contain a hollow cavity lined with natural deep purple quartz stone clusters, vintage and collectable Hawaiian shirts that had coconut buttons, vibrant prints of palm trees and sunset aloha floral color palette, turquoise jewelry with stone-to-stone inlay in a wide array of colors and matrices. I had a section for Native American turquoise rings, necklaces and bracelets with symbols of sun, moon, stars, feathers and turtles. Each symbol serving as a connection to ancestral wisdom and traditions passed down through the generations.

In Bernalillo, New Mexico I rented a house from Robert, a man who arranged to send woven hand crafted colorful Guatemalan indigenous traditional clothing known as traje, a culturally rich aspect of Guatemalan identity from an ancient Mayan population. There were huipils (blouses), cortes (skirts), fajas (belts). The traje is not just clothing; it's a symbol of Guatemalan heritage having color patterns and a weaving technique specific to each region and community. The blouses or tunics were decorated with intricate patterns and symbols, the long wraparound skirts were all handwoven, and the brightly colored belts cinching the waist added to the overall design. The traje is deeply rooted in Mayan culture often retelling stories and legends that people enjoyed hearing. I loved sharing the cultural heritage of the clothing and the symbolic meanings embedded in each garment.

My market table also included beautiful hand-dyed woven wool Bolivian rugs created by master weavers. Several of the Sufi community in Torreon, New Mexico imported large hand puppets that initially I sold on street corners in Manhattan and then included in the wares to decorate the booths I designed for craft fairs and the markets.

People came to the flea market in Tesuque, New Mexico to talk with me each week, whether I sold imported prayer rugs, clothing from Guatemala, or handcrafted puppets. They arrived weekly for conversation to continue the dialogue from the previous weekend and bought whatever I had on my artistically arranged table. I was comfortably alive with the recognition that this is my particular craft—intimate conversation—my work and purpose, the joy of being present to the moment, regardless to what it's named and how many degrees are posted after my name, or whether it happens in an office building or my home, on the beach, at a table displaying crafts, through a telephone line or on the streets of New York; whether it's called therapy or psychology or spiritual conversation or flea market craft fair vendor. This is how I be: teaching, speaking, rubbing hearts, living into the smile. An invitation to mutual vulnerability.

Clarifying our understanding of simple words will not just change our way of speaking; it will also change our way of thinking and change our basic feelings—we are recreated. When I speak with another being who is similar to me, yet different, I begin not only to understand the other, but also to understand what I myself am speaking about. —Adin Steinsaltz

A gateway to discovery: speaking, being witnessed, to become visible, finding words, a voice for our secrets and narrative. I became a bridge that is tentatively walked, to show up, meet and greet the other as self. Bear witness, losing self and personality, your story my story, two hearts rubbing in this moment and continuing. We come alive in true conversation, our willingness to be seen, to listen and speak.

Those who love the world serve it. To share what you have been given. —Andrew Harvey

Location shifts to Haulover beach in South Florida. I encounter people in the ocean, and the conversation continues. Do I get paid for those sessions—not always financially—yet the encounters make my heart sing. Walking in the ocean I nod and sometimes pause to enter a conversation—who are you standing in our holy body of sea, who am I as I walk in the current of mother ocean.

Who is wise? The person who learns from everyone. Who is strong? The person who has control over his/her passions. Who is honored? The person who honors others. And who is rich? The person who is satisfied with what he/she has. —the Talmud

What is our work, that occupies a major portion of our life: whether I be named doctor, waitress, parent, a financier, garbage collector, flea market vendor, meditation or yoga teacher, politician, chef, librarian, or artist. These are strategies to learn to remember ourselves, devices when used well to awaken, scenarios to not become enamored with the form; many are the services and possibilities offered to humanity, the structures to make money to continue paying and living a responsible life, as we gift our heart, live into our smile.

The shop-foreman, irritation showing plainly on his face, strode over to Jules, a non-conforming free spirit. 'Listen,' he growled, 'do me and everyone else in the shop a big favor and quit whistling while you are here at this job.' Surprised, Jules replied, 'who is working at a job? Whatever I have done in my life, it is not a job.' This is the way I am, It's not a business; it's the way I am. This is what's happening.' —Osho

- Amma
"Love is the only medicine that can heal the wounds of the world."

Section Thirty-Two:
I Remember

For memory is a blessing: it creates bonds rather than destroys them. Bonds between present and past. It is because I remember our common beginning that I move closer to my fellow human beings. It is because I refuse to forget that their future is as important as my own. To forget is to deny ourself.

It is the obligation to remember that drives me to take pen in hand and write one word after another. I ask myself what the opposite of memory is. The opposite of memory is the sickness of forgetting, what today we call Alzheimer's Disease. My message is simple. Never fight against memory. Even if it is painful, it will help you; it will give you something; it will enrich you. Ultimately, what would culture be without memory? What would be love for a friend without remembering that love the next day? One cannot live without it. One cannot exist without remembrance. —Elie Wiesel

To live as an active agent creating change in this world is our obligation and moral responsibility—we may be powerless to erase the violence and wars that erupt throughout the world; our humanity is based on the ability to remember the past, to never forget, to remember those who are denied the right to dissent, that all people have a right to live harmoniously. Memory is the ground for peace. To remember those who have perished, keeping memory alive is to not be an accomplice to injustice, humiliation and violation. Let us garden integrity, take action and oppose indifference, apathy and inattentiveness. The quality of our life rests on this, of awakening into love in this lifetime!

Remembering is an act of love. Not to turn away, to step into the current of life. To remember and to breathe the mystery, holding the miraculous—we inhabit memory as a living presence. Love blossoms as we diminish the personal, seeing through the eyes of the heart; awakening to love as the soul of the universe, to our true nature, embracing our world with love.

There is a beautiful teaching: before we are born, still in our mother's womb, an angel holds a light shining it over our head and the whole universe can now be seen offering us a vision of all past and future events. And then months later, before we are born and arrive into this world, the angel of oblivion appears and lightly taps baby us on the mouth creating philtrum, the vertical groove in our upper lip that runs from the nose to the top of the lip. We now forget everything we knew and enter into this life. In the spiritual context a philtrum is a symbol of connection to the divine, a reminder of our spiritual journey—a mark of a divine touch, a location where spiritual energies converge. The angel of conception silences our knowledge of the secrets of the universe. Life is to remember what we already knew. To sharpen and refine our memory, strip away the accoutrements, distractions, beliefs, to cut through all views and answers here in our ordinary life. Listen inwardly to what we already know. Remember!

If a person permits their soul to listen, the soul will soon learn that all it needs to do is remember. Because in some dim and enigmatic way, it already knows all this.
—Reb Adin Steinsaltz

Close relatives of mine have struggled and eventually lost their location of time and space, their knowingness of the what is and what has been. To recognize this deterioration, the progression and slow decline in memory, thinking, reasoning and personality changes have brought me to look at each family member with a new eye, with questions.

My sister and mother and my mother's side of the family often forced their world to be shaped by their wishes rather than by the what is. Rarely were my mother's family members interested in looking directly at life with her hardships, to use the circumstances as they appeared and then release them. There was often an invention and twist to the truth of life—its risks and uncertainty. I have few answers many questions as I currently listen to my sisters struggles to hold on to the form and sequence of her life. I have remained open free of knowing as they struggled to gain a clarity that was not originally part of their daily routine. They all carried a social dignity paramount to how they have lived. What's right and looks socially proper/acceptable were high on their list of importance.

There is a parable about a just woman, a teacher named Ruth, who came to the city of Babylon. Seeing that the people were immoral and sinful, unkind and corrupt Ruth was determined to liberate the people, to save them from their unkindness and cruelty. Daily she walked the street protesting, speaking about integrity, opposing corruption and greed, lies and hypocrisy. In the beginning people listened, finding Ruth amusing and entertaining. Eventually they stopped listening, lost interest, were no longer entertained and so they continued in their apathy, their indifference to others suffering. Propriety and social acceptance mattered more to the people of Babylon than personal integrity and kindness. One day a young person, moved by compassion towards Ruth approached her and said: *Don't you see how hopeless this is to speak up and try to change oblivious cruel people?* Ruth replied: *In the beginning when I first arrived here I did imagine I could change people, today I know that I can't. Yet if I continue to speak up, to speak out, to point out the lack of kindness and corruption as a continuous teaching, it's to prevent them from ultimately changing me!*

Courage to be oneself, to not indulge mindless entertainment and external stimulus, ultimately to find a deep

sense of meaning beyond distracting ourselves with pleasure, to sit in grief for the worlds woundings and losses,
a reverence for the beauty of life in our understanding
that all of us are part of the web of life, to remember
what matters, what's meaningful, to retain wonder and
joy—to hold both the dark and the light and here we are.

Life shrinks or expands in proportion to one's courage.
—Anais Nin

I remember our childhood. My sister Iris was com-
pliant, obeyed rules, studied hard to get decent grades,
restrained, sulky and pouty, dependent, non-resistant
allowing most anyone to make her decisions and take care
of many things. On the other hand, I was disobedient,
defiant, sweet, happy, resisted authority, smart, rarely
studied, barely passed my grades, often late for school,
noncompliant, independent, singing from the moment I
woke up although I did not like to get up early and loved
to stay up late, weakened immune system from childhood
illness of scarlet fever, eye surgery and tons of antibiotics.

Sing in the morning and cry at night I was told by Adele,
my mother, as I walked around the house singing. *Can't
you make your mother happy* was the directive told to me,
and the inner meaning was: give up your independence
and enthusiastic spirit and obey. No, I didn't!

Iris and I are currently moved into recognizable versions of our younger self. Me, a matured version of what

my earlier teacher, Jean called a mischievous cherub, although I also now include seeing myself as quietly inner often peaceful grateful privileged to be alive with the work I cherish, continuing to speak up as I experience injustice, to keep questions alive, and Iris with full time attendants at Orchard Cove a skilled nursing memory care unit with twenty-four hour attendants. Are these formulas for an aging clear mind, a preclude for dementia and Alzheimer's—unproven possibilities!

Be hopeful, be optimistic, Never, ever be afraid to make some noise and get in good trouble, necessary trouble.
—John Lewis

In my investigation memory loss comes into being through unhappiness, dependency, a distorted mindset that prefers living in illusions inventing a reality that soothes, that fosters drama, rather than the truth to how life really is as well as conditions that don't bring proper oxygen to the brain, a degree of genetics—that prefers living in exile as a stranger to ourself, seeing others as the stranger, garnering versions that reflect a culture that turns away from inner inquiry corrupting the discovery of personal identity.

Happiness and independence, living on the edge, inner entertainment, allowing the world to come and go–no separation—living into the oneness, this might be an antidote, a remedy to hold the mind accountable, to living mentally sound and intact.

*A full inhabitation of memory makes human beings
conscious, a living connection between what has been,
what is and what is about to be. Robbed of our memory
by Alzheimer's or by a stroke, we lose our identities.
Memory is the living link to personal freedom.*
—David Whyte

And so memory, our anchor, expands a spiritual leap
into the unknown, a mirror to magnify each other's light
and transform difficulties into a deeper capacity to love.
We are directed to create spaces in the world building a
personal sanctuary to reveal what already exists. Every
moment is infused with divinity and our work is to strip
away the distractions and obstructions, allowing true
essence to emerge. To be present and remember is to be
human.

*Without memory, our existence would be barren and
opaque, like a prison cell into which no light penetrates.
Because I remember, I despair. Because I remember,
I have the duty to reject despair.* —Elie Wiesel

Section Thirty-Three: Israel

The miracle of a small country with large spirit, child of hope, created to be a light unto other nations has been a force in my life. Age seventeen I traveled to Israel and lived in a kibbutz, a communal settlement, meeting many young people with generous great-hearted dreams. One eighteen year old boy imagining that his Jewish community in South Africa would soon be persecuted was striving to create a safe prosperous place for Jewish people living in his African community was diligently working to airlift families to come live in Israel. Large dreams extending beyond any I had imagined: I was inspired.

I love the land, the energy, the dreams and possibilities and might have remained if my mother hadn't insisted I return to the United States to attend college. In fact she managed to have the American Embassy find and fly me back to Rhode Island. And that began my long college adventures, originating with Emerson College in Boston, Massachusetts.

Initially I supported Student Zionist activities until many years later when the dream again arose refueling hope for this small country. Hatikvah, national anthem of Israel, *the Hope*. As long as the heart beats within us may our hearts beat both for ourselves and the world we are striving to repair.

As long as the heart within The soul yearns, our hope is not yet lost. The hope that is two thousand years old to be a free nation in our land the land of Zion and Jerusalem.
—Hatikva-Nafatali Herz Imber, Israel national anthem

This dream lay fallow in my heart, her seeds planted early on when I lived at Kibbutz Ein Hashlosha in the Eshkol region, close to the Gaza Strip, experiencing a special collective community that's particular to Israel. The kibbutz is a uniquely Israeli phenomenon with a cultural legacy and an important role in the nation's history. The word, *kibbutz,* means *gathering* in Hebrew; originally they were exercises in radical democracy. Following the threads of our life is a love letter to self and aging offers this rich possibility to watch the planted seeds grow.

Each of us has a divine name. Mindfulness is the key to unlocking its secret. The term in the Talmud for mindfulness is kavanat lev, the directing of the heart. Real mindfulness comes about by directed compassion, a softening of our awareness, a loving embrace of our lives, a soft letting be. —Alan Lew

Israel holds a sense of the sacred and the practices, tradition and holiness opened me to the ways of the world, to humanity; the world is our true family. To experience the oneness, the interconnectedness of all beings, to become a divine instrument is to turn towards the world. And so I listen, pay attention to a beautiful land that captured my heart and sensibilities, and I pay homage, bow down to a powerful experience that directed and inspired me along this continuing journey.

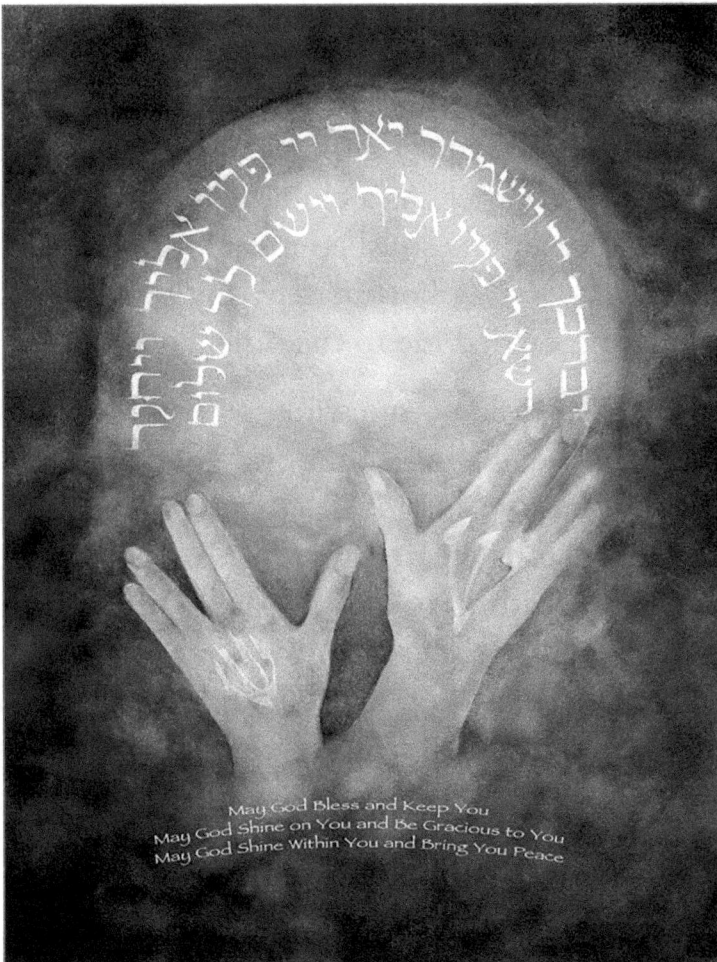

May God Bless and Keep You
May God Shine on You and Be Gracious to You
May God Shine Within You and Bring You Peace

Section Thirty-Four: Awakening

Only that day dawns to which we are awake.
—Henry David Thoreau

I love words, a good conversation, unanswerable questions, conversations with four-leggeds, with a star, the sun and moon, a sheet of paper, a song, the ocean, a book and with another. As a child, words held power to reveal meaning. Adults shushed me a lot. *Don't say that, don't ask that, shhhhh.* Fortunately, my sense of humor and risk taking carried me to the other side of longing.

I persisted to ask, to question, to listen, to observe and feel. I see that feelings come and go, that to become a mature human is a long walk, that being visible takes courage, that words create a beautiful shelter as well as opening doors leading to and from the heart, that suffering is inevitable in fact endemic to the experience of being alive, that maturity, wisdom and joy are available, that life is a precious opportunity, that integrity does not have a price tag. And so I speak words, I write words, service in the name of love. Here to awaken!

I have come not to teach but to awaken.
—Meher Baba

And from the tender child to this adult in her eighties I have carried the fire of longing, the fuel of witnessing, the question of life and death. One generation to the next—continuation. With clarity, with awareness life becomes vast and we awaken. To be in this world willing to grieve—to offer inspiration, be of service mindful towards ourself, all essential requirements.

In earlier years I did not include myself in the equation. That's a huge lie, we are not free to be of true service before we attend to the more difficult job of being available to our own true self. To initially feed and replenish our own joys and sorrows.

Putting your total energy into awakening, from this place see awareness as a question of life and death, then we are alive and life continues growing bigger and more vast. Seeing with clarity, wake up ! And your whole life will be transformed. —Osho

I do not want my fire to go out. When personal suffering is dropped this life can be used in a more effective manner. Awakening is available regardless to external circumstances in our life, in the midst of the flow of our life.

Now to live this endless process of discovery. Awakening is a shift of our identity, and what have we to offer more than ourself? We feel life itself. That is essentially who I am. Our shift of identity effects the world, it informs the world. Awakened consciousness—we see ourselves as light and that allows us to see the divinity, the divine spark in everyone. Now to relate to this vision, that love. This is the ground, a foundation for a deeper way of being. We are called to wake up. Embrace this!

It's a drum and arms waving. It's a bonfire on the top edge of a hill, this meeting again with you. That's the embrace we want, a place where great souls can stop and rest. —Rumi

Section Thirty-Five: Music

Many say that life entered the human body by the help of music, but the truth is that life itself is music.
—Hafiz

*A*sanctuary and refuge, music lives in the present moment appearing under all circumstances. A perfect partner as I write entering the world of sound. Music, morning and night: with dinner at home, mornings accompanying breakfast, daily as I write, Friday night and Saturday a musical Shabbos, when I am happy as well as sad, tired or energized, the expanse is immense. Music is food for the soul.

My favorite piece of music is the one we hear all the time if we are quiet. —John Cage

Our life has a rhythm that connects music to the heartbeat, to our breath. And we are connected, affecting health, moods, life inside us. Music is sound and rhythm and to be sensitive to the variety is to know what sounds irritate, unsettle our nerves, allows music/sound to be used well and become a source of harmonious healing and joy. Always shifting and changing like the ocean clouds and sky. As the sunset turns to twilight in the silence of the darkness this world of flowers and fragrance carries sounds that reflect the heavens, echo the magnificence of the earth.

Whenever you talk without singing, you are
disconnecting yourself from the creation of the world.
—Rebbe Nachman

Music unites. Yes, we sing, play instruments, chant bhajan, songs, kirtan, nigunim, wordless melodies, devotional music. Practices to expand the spirit. And so it has been my inclination from younger years through to now to listen/sing in and with communities that are predominately musical.

Music has been instrumental in quieting thoughts and mental activity in my life. I discovered this using music while writing. Like a beautiful meditation exercise ringing bells in my heart, not a ripple as I drop into the tune of inner silence. The greatest device I have found to drop into awareness is music and movement, and they go together. Listening to the inner music that is already there. Like a boat taking us to the beyond.

There's a song that wants to sing itself through us. We
just have to be available. Maybe the song that is to be
sung through us is the most beautiful requiem for an
irreplaceable planet or maybe it's a song of joyous rebirth
as we create a new culture that doesn't destroy its world.
—Joanna Macy

This love affair, hearing the beloved in the atmosphere is the last sense to leave as we are dying. The auditory system is connected to the brain stem which controls breathing and heartbeat, the dying brain responds to sound tones even during an unconscious state. Hearing is the last sense to go in the dying process.

In music there are moments of 'rest' of no sound. That space between notes is powerful, meaningful. It is more eloquent than any sound. —Thich Nhat Hahn

Silence can be touched through musical notes. Heightening our sensitivity, entering a world of harmony—this is the place where the music never stops. Tucked within our own true selves, bringing us home into this universe—we become the music. The sound between the notes fill us, reverberates to return to the sound that shatters as well as to the silence: both are the root of our being.

It acts like love—music, it reaches toward the face, touches it, and tries to let you know His promise: that all will be okay. It acts like love—music, and tells the feet, 'You do not have to be so burdened.' My body is covered with wounds this world made, but I still longed to kiss Him, even when God said, 'Could you also kiss the hand that caused each scar, for you will not find me until you do.' It does that—music—helps us to forgive.
—Rabia of Basra

Section Thirty-Six:
This Now

*As I get older I am turning into myself. Now layers of
time live in me. I think of this layering as vertical time,
when all time flows into the present moment. Time
is not something I have; it's what I'm made up of.*
—Susan Moon

And I wanted to awaken: to love, to lighten the
suffering in this world, to live in visibility of the
ocean, to be satisfied, in wonder, to practice and wake
up. And here I be—quietly reflective, writing, listening,
aging, privileged this continuation, in true conversation,
the work of this lifetime, each day a surprise. Wounded
I hold the brokenness even share it with the ocean always
freshly renewed through our tears. Tiny fish bump against
my feet as I walk to her music, this orchestra of nonresis-
tance. Unguarded I walk, a troubadour of courtly love I
serenade the song-meisters to encourage a beautiful day.

Paying attention to this remarkable aging process—
everyone is easily able to be young, yet few of us are privileged to grow old. I study those who have maintained
clarity of brain/mind. My 107 year old neighbor, the 106
year old mother of Temple Israel's secretary, my 98 year
old cousin Henry Bromberg and his 90 year wife Arlene

in Fort Lauderdale; always to investigate and question: is there a formula for living/aging well? Open and joyful are essential ingredients for heartfelt longevity. The other is non-compliance/independence. Not allowing others to infiltrate with the agenda to do for me what I can do for myself.

Elie Wiesel, when asked for personal forgiveness towards his murdered community replied: *I am a witness, I do not think that forgiveness is relevant, not forgetting—that is relevant. With the passage of time we must recalibrate, that's a far stretch from forgiveness. It's as close as we can get.*

I cherish the power of memory in this present moment. We are an archive, a personal amulet and link to preserving culture. And all of this in the present moment: that we continue to remember saturates and suffuses our life, carries us from the mundane to the ethereal.

Echoes and whispers, to offer attention to what we are named at birth. *A dying man takes his soul with him but leaves his name to the survivors,* says Gavriel, the protagonist in Wiesel's novel *The Gates of the Forest.* And so we have echoes in the present moment of redemptive memories, of history, to carry holiness into the profane, into each present moment.

While we are custodians of our memories, our own experience is the real. The evidence of our personal history lies in how we are living our life now. We carry the blemishes as well as the hopes of the ancestors. We celebrate history while being sensitive to it at the same time, letting go of narrow views where privilege is not for the few, where we are not indifferent to global suffering, and are all answerable to humanity, open to universal oneness in this present moment.

Pretend you are an old man/woman watching children play. Just watch, delighted, even though you know the obstacles, the heartbreaks, the sorrows, the jolts. You know these things. Now is your time to stand at the edge and watch the water flow by. Just watch, without getting caught in the current. —Yongey Mingyur Rinpoche

Section Thirty-Seven: Death

Death is our eternal companion... It is always to our left, at an arm's length... It has always been watching you. It always will until the day it taps you. The thing to do when you're impatient is... to turn to your left and ask advice from your death. An immense amount of pettiness is dropped if your death makes a gesture to you, or if you catch a glimpse of it, or if you just catch the feeling that your companion is there watching you.
—Carlos Castaneda

*M*y dear friend contacted me last night, she is entering palliative care opting to forego any further treatment as she chooses: *Best enjoy this time with my beloved. Deeply feeling calm and knowing this life was worth living. I am in no need of grief and inspiration, wouldn't mind an intelligent joke now and then. Joy seems to be working. Constant wee miracles. I wish the same for you.* —Elaine

I also remember how many friends and family had to relocate their brain into distorted reality before leaving their body. Often wandering into confusion, sadness, anger and grief. I pay attention to walking my friend Elaine home. So personal our choices into the unknown.

Life in a body has its limit, called death—we arrive into this world as a continuation; the illusion of permanence cultivates a suffering that fills this world. The greatest mystery of life is not life itself, it's death. This daily experience with impermanence, emphasized by loss, brings us to know what endures. To consider how to use this precious time. Life and death cannot be separated, they are aspects of each other. *There is no one exempt. Before death we are all equal.* When we ask: for *whom the bell tolls,* we are forgetting the endless extravagance of life— the continual renewal of seasons, from summer to winter to spring.

We cannot prevent death, no-one is exempt and we are reminded of the design, the order of each generation yielding to death so that children and grandchildren step forward in the order of life, like rotating orderly seasons.

The bad news is that you are falling through the air, there is nothing to hang onto and you have no parachute. The good news is that there is no ground.
—Chogyan Trungpa Rinppoche

I recall the parable of the heartbroken mother who asked a shamanic healer to restore life to her recently deceased child. She was tasked with finding a mustard seed from a home that has never experienced death. Relieved as she knew how plentiful and inexpensive mustard seeds are, the cheapest spice available, and she knew that most every house in the village would have some. She knocked on many doors, visited most every household in her village and soon discovered that each household was touched by mortality, that all have experienced loss and death, that she was not alone in her grief, that the universe was not singling her out for a special punishment, that she was one among most families who death has visited, leading her to truly understand that all living beings are subject to death. She attentively, lovingly carried her child to be buried with her heart no longer disturbed, open to grieve her loss, knowing that the body is not eternal and that the memory of her beautiful child survives.

She returned to the shamanic healer to find solace in understanding the universal nature of impermanence, the fragility of life. The healer explained that for each of us birth and death cannot be avoided, are a reality for all. Years passed and she eventually became part of the healing community, compassionate and appreciating the privilege of this life and the value of living wholeheartedly in sacred awareness. Time passed and aging the woman gathered her extended family the villagers as they talked and sang and danced with her far into the night.

How does one become a butterfly? Pooh asked pensively. *You must want to fly so much that you're willing to give up being a caterpillar,* Piglet replied. *You mean you die?* asked Pooh. *Yes and no,* he answered. *What looks like you will die, but what's really you will live on.*
—A.A. Milne

Death is a great teacher, directing us to pay attention. How to have a relationship to what is never born, never dies, and therein lies the innumerable deaths in life that accompany us on our journey. Through self-recognition comes a remarkable teaching that all things remain alive and present, the reality of life and death continuously meet in the heart, in the heart of life.

Our dead are never dead to us, until we have forgotten them. —George Eliot

Poet Andrea Gibson invited the world to *raise what will end you, with love.* To cherish, to embrace both our mortality and impermanence. All the beloveds—all of us part of one body, called humanity:

When death first came to visit, I refused to let her enter my home. She sat outside in the garden picking buttercups, painting her face the color of the sun. I stood at the window for hours watching her, thinking Why is she still here? It's not like she has nowhere to go. I'd try to sleep, but as soon as I closed my eyes I would hear her outside talking daisies into blooming at night. I suspect she knew, I too am the type to open my petals for the moon. On my eighth night awake, I did it—I walked out to the garden and invited her in. I poured her a cup of lavender tea. I made up her bed and turned down the lights. I wished her good dreams, though I knew her good dream was to one day take my life.

*I used to believe I knew my purpose, thought for sure
I understood my calling. But my calling, I now know,
has always been this: to parent my own departure. To
keep a roof over the head of the truth. To raise what
will end me, with love.... I'll be ready, I promise. I've
committed the rest of my days to learning how to give
you my blessings.... I know it's how you say I love you.
I know others will hear it as a curse and try to rinse
your mouth out with soap. But I will hear your I love
you. I will hear it so clearly my last words will be I love
you too, as I watch you make something of yourself, as I
open my petals for the moon.*

—Andrea Gibson

Section Thirty-Eight: Prayer

Pray for Peace

Pray to whomever you kneel down to:
Jesus nailed to his wooden or plastic cross,
His suffering face bent to kiss you,
Buddha still under the bo tree in scorching heat.
Adonoi, Allah. Raise your arms to Mary
That she may lay her palm on our brows,
To Shekinah, Queen of Heaven and Earth,
To Inanna in her stripped descent.
Then pray to the bus driver who takes you to work.
On the bus, pray for everyone riding buses all over the world.
Drop some silver and pray.
Waiting in line for the movies, for the ATM,
For your latte and croissant, offer your plea.
Make your eating and drinking a supplication,
Make your slicing of carrots a holy act,
Each translucent layer of the onion, a deeper prayer.
To Hawk or Wolf, or the Great Whale, pray.
Bow down to terriers and shepherds and Siamese cats.
Fields of artichokes and elegant strawberries.
Make the brushing of your hair
A prayer, every strand its own voice,

Singing in the choir on your head.
As you wash your face, the water slipping
Through your fingers, a prayer: Water,
Softest thing on earth, gentleness
That wears away rock.
Making love, of course, is already prayer.
Skin, and open mouths worshipping that skin,
The fragile cases we are poured into.
If you're hungry, pray. If you're tired.
Pray to Gandhi and Dorothy Day.
Shakespeare. Sappho. Sojourner Truth.
When you walk to your car, to the mailbox,
To the video store, let each step
be a prayer that we all keep our legs,
That we do not blow off anyone else's legs.
Or crush their skulls.
And if you are riding on a bicycle
Or a skateboard, in a wheelchair, each revolution
Of the wheels a prayer as the earth revolves:
Less harm, less harm, less harm.
And as you work, typing with a new manicure,
A tiny palm tree painted on one pearlescent nail,
Or delivering soda or drawing good blood
Into rubber-capped vials, twirling pizzas—
With each breath in, take in the faith of those
Who have believed when belief seemed foolish,
Who persevered. With each breath out, cherish.
Pull weeds for peace, turn over in your sleep for peace,
Feed the birds, each shiny seed

That spills onto the earth, another second of peace.
Wash your dishes, call your mother, drink wine.
Shovel leaves or snow or trash from your sidewalk.
Make a path. Fold a photo of a dead child
Around your Visa card. Scoop your holy water
From the gutter. Gnaw your crust.
Mumble along like a crazy person, stumbling
Your prayer through the streets.

—Ellen Bass

Now to sing, love and celebration in our world of darkness and light. Each cry of the heart penetrates above and below in this dance of the beyond. *The soul evolves not by addition but subtraction,* said Meister Eckhart and our open heart moves us to the simple altar of oneness, raising holy sparks. Heaven and earth are interconnected and love dispels all illusions of separateness. For every word I write a word in the heavens is inscribed. Every place we stand is holy, and so what's in our heart, the stillness inside; even to recite one word with loving intention, the quality of the intention creates sacred space.

Thank You

Heart, you are lost: but there's a path from the lover to love, hidden but visible. Worlds blaze round you. Don't shrink; the path's hidden, and yours. —Rumi

Remembering and celebrating the beautiful hearts that have taken flight: petals released, your fragrance continues to inspire and teach: Bonnie Whittingham, Dr. Harriet Rose Meiss, Beth Weiner, Mary Glassman, Adele and Manuel Bromberg, Reb Zalman Schachter-Shalomi, Jean Robertson, Dr. Janine Canan, Dr. Rona Lieberman, Joan Holode, Marcia Fein, Dr. Marsha Woolf, Heidi Kingsbury, Reshad Feild, Thich Nhat Hahn, Dr. Elisabeth Kubler-Ross, Sandesh, Taffy Manuelian, Adnan Sarhan, Andrea Dworkin, Elaine Marchese. Walking each other home.

Giving thanks to everything that brought me to this moment.

To Alexandra: this wonderful holy dance, my beloved companion, your happiness seeing me eases earth plane discomfort, innocence for this well worn simple soul, a beautiful face through all seasons. Loving in our extended walk/dance together. The language of the heart has infinite wisdom.

I wish I could show you when you are lonely or in darkness The astonishing light of your own being!

To Scott: your hope for the children is remarkable, inspiring vision and a promise, your presence in my life lights my heart.

To the Bromberg family: Arlene, Henry and Laura who offer inclusive loving-kindness.

To Linda: certainly we have walked this walk many times: friend, voice on the telephone, dependable: a friend for all time.

Leslie Landy, for being a reliable steady source of wisdom and common sense. Your loving-kindness is immense—a true healer, I am grateful.

To Deborah: for listening. And your appreciation for the writing. An admirable gift and quality. Thank you.

The Santa Fe, New Mexico family: Helga, Simcha and Ambika: our love adventures paved the way.

To the magnificent teachers whose breath have ignited my fire, this circle of lovers who sat with me—what a lucky lifetime to have been embraced by such awakenings: Jean Robertson, Kabir Helminski, Elisabeth Kubler-Ross, Adyshanti, GangaJi, Adnan Sarhan, Thich Nhat Hahn, Mother Meera, Ram Dass, Ammachi, Reb Zalman Schacter-Sholomi, Reshad Feild, Reb David Ingber, Yogi Bhajan, Natalie Goldberg, Ma Jaya Bhagavati, Krishnamurti, Eve Ensler, Chris Griscom, Deva Premal and Miten, Andrea Dworkin.

And always the voices through the telephone lines, the beloveds, who in vulnerability bring life stories, exchanging uplifted energy, a shared self-inquiry, a lotus to us both this remarkable privilege, relationships with purpose, spiritual conversations, this miraculous work.

Open the Treasure Chest

Writing is the act of discovery Know that you will eventually have to leave everything behind. The writing will demand it of you. Writers are great lovers. They fall in love with other writers. That's how they learn to write. They take on a writer, read everything by him or her, read it over again until they understand how the writer moves, pauses and sees. That's what being a lover is: stepping out of yourself, stepping into someone else's skin. As writers we live twice, like a cow that eats its food, and then regurgitates it to chew and digest it again. We have a second chance at biting into our experience and examining it. —Natalie Goldberg

The following writers/books capture my heart:

Pico Iyer: *The Art of Stillness, Aflame*

Ruchira Avatar Adi Da Samraj: *What, Where, When, How, Why, and Who To Remember To Be Happy*

David Whyte: *Crossing the Unknown Sea, Consolations 1 , Consolations 2*

Natalie Goldberg: *Three Simple Lines, Writing Down the Bones*

Daniel Ladinsky: *The Subject Tonight is Love, The Gift, The Purity of Desire, A Year With Hafiz, Love Poems from God*

P.D. Ouspenski: *Strange Life of Ivan Osokin*

Alan Lew: *One God Clapping, This is Real and You Are Completely Unprepared, Be Still and Get Going*

Katherine Thanas: *The Truth of This Life*

Joan Halifax: *Standing at the Edge, The Fruitful Darkness*

Charlotte Joko: *Everyday Zen, Ordinary Wonder*

Norman Fischer: *The World Could Be Otherwise, When You Greet Me I bow*

Dr. Paula Bromberg: *Notes From the Ocean,* and *The Way of the Lover, Being Eighty*

Thich Nhat Hahn: *True Love, The Art of Communicating, Silence*

Trina Paulus: *Hope for the Flowers*

Tzvi Freeman: *Bringing Heaven Down to Earth*

Elie Wiesel: *From the Kingdom of Memory, Open Heart*

Bernie Glassman: *Bearing Witness*

Yongey Mingyur Rinpoche: *In Love With The World*

Rami Shapiro: *Hasidic Tales, And You Shall Love*

Chris Griscom: *Ocean Born*

Yaffa Eliach, *Hasidic Tales of the Holocaust*

Margery Williams: *The Velveteen Rabbit*

Florence Caplow, Susan Moon: *The Hidden Lamp*

Andrea Gibson: *You Better Be Lightening, Lord of the Butterflies*

Oscar Wilde: *The Happy Prince, The Selfish Giant*

Curt Leviant: *The Man Who Thought He Was Messiah*

Cooper Edens: *Caretaker of Wonder, If You're Afraid of the Dark Remember the Night Rainbow*

Ariel Burger: *Witness*

Delphine Horvilleur: *Living with our Dead*

Meher Baba: *Life at Its Best*

Arthur Kurzweil: *On the Road with Rabbi Steinsaltz*

Ranier Maria Rilke: *On Love and Other Difficulties*

Books are the carriers of civilization. Without books, history is silent, literature dumb, science crippled, thought and speculation at a standstill. Without books the development of a civilization would have been impossible. They are the engines of change, windows on the world, lighthouses erected in the sea of time. They are the companions, teachers, magicians, bankers of the treasures of the mind. Books are humanity in print.
—Barbara Tuchman

Singing Creation Into Being

Always the Music

Whenever you speak without singing, you are disconnecting yourself from creation. —Reb Nachman

There is a story that in the highest heaven there is a sanctuary, a sacred and joyful paradise that song alone can unlock. Music is the key to open the gates. Music stirs whatever lies in the heart. The mixture of devotion, sensuality, passion and pleasure come forward as our inner being is moved by what has been called *the language of the angels.*

Universal language, music reveals the voice of our soul. The sound between the notes fill us, reverberate to return to the silence which is the root of our being. The music is the magic, inspiration the rhythm composition and harmony, bringing aliveness to each moment, offering stamina and life force. Music lives in the present moment. The sound between the notes fill us, reverberate to return to the silence which is the root of our being.

The following are a few of the musicians and music that uplift my spirit:

Deva Premal and Miten   *Leonard Cohen*

David Darling   *Luciano Pavarotti*

Maria Callas

Cantor Azi Schwartz

Hebrew Synagogue music

Yiddish songs

The Ocean

Gregorian Chants

Broadway Musicals

Jerusalema, Zulu song
    from South Africa

Giacomo Puccini

There's a music for everything. Didn't you ever hear the earth spinning? It makes a sound like a humming top. Dear me, yes! Everything in the world—trees, rocks and stars and human beings—they all have their own true music. —P.L. Travers

Further Continuing Work

Telephone sessions, E-mail and texts are available for self-study, inner investigation and personal growth. Mindful conversation, finding our voice our joy and sorrow brings deeper understanding enabling us to develop our practice of presence and live free from habituated conditioned patterns awakening to the sacred mystery of being. Contact through E-mail or Facebook:

Dr. Paula Bromberg

Goldoceandrive@gmail.com

Facebook: PaulaAmbikaBromberg

About the Author

Dr. Paula Bromberg: Psychologist, Teacher, writer, lover of life, ocean-walker, inspired by her personal journey has experienced many paths, teachers, spiritual communities and methods. Notes from the Ocean draws on direct experience—both professional encounters and years of walking, singing in beautiful oceans and beaches throughout the world. Her books are written through an understanding that comes from decades of study, teaching, intimate conversation and digesting life experiences. Traveling and receiving initiation into Eastern and Western lineages: Sufi, Buddhist, Jewish, Gurdjieffian, East Indian; learning within living traditions, transcending formal boundaries to teach from those places and kindle a fire in the heart of others.

The author has a Doctorate in Philosophy in Clinical Psychology maintains a current telephone practice, recorded a live television series *Conversations with Dr Paula*. Her books, *The Way of the Lover, A Way of Understanding, The Fifth Way—Life at its Best* and *Notes from the Ocean, A Celebration of Love* are the foundation of her work. The living interconnectedness makes up the real world and all traditions are part of this way of being in the world. The creative force is love.

Paula was on the faculty of Northern New Mexico College co-creating and teaching the first University program with Dr. Elisabeth Kubler-Ross to educate and train hospice workers. She was interviewed and recorded by Dr. Zoe Lewis as a guest on her radio show *Health Through Knowledge*. As a consultant and frequent speaker for a regenerative medicine television series *My Medicine TV*, Dr. Bromberg also pioneered her own TV show *Conversations with Dr. Paula*.

She developed and created a psychological/spiritual system throughout her more than fifty years of working in conversation with people. To discover and study our essential nature; to experience the meaning and purpose of our life awakens us through concrete teachings that transform us to live our life mindfully, with presence. It is our birthright to be initiated into the truths that evoke the powers of our natural gifts enabling us to find hidden meaning and higher guidance inherent in our life.

From an early age Dr. Paula demonstrated an irrepressible striving to understand and to awaken. A voice of clarity and presence of heart Paula has written remarkable books of timeless wisdom that will change your life. Her work and writings have been praised by many of the foremost spiritual leaders from numerous traditions.

Dr. Paula says: *Personal identity appeared impossible— before I understood to be in the world and not of it. Form became a pliable construct, with the edges often bending and dropping away. Years passing by mirrors, no reflection, driven to move this body until collapsed into exhaustion; passionate; initiated into invisibility, invisible threads, silver chord to the moon. Little sleep or rest. Years of practice to create a witness, someone home while dancing through this perilous wonder is the rope that tethered/tethers me from this heart to the heart of the universe. A devotee to Love, walking with the beloveds who dare risk and shatter form. This private experience, passionate, at times troublesome—living on the edge sometimes out of the margin, at times negligent to holding humanity in a container of love, I was protected throughout gathering experiences being in adventures and always the call to awaken as the greatest possibility—through a body that was driven to wake up.*

May this book offer that vision of a universe created with and for love.

Stay close to everything that makes you glad that you are alive. Bring your cup near me, for a drink from Love's Hands. So I will always lean my heart as close to your soul as I can. —Hafiz

The Game

To penetrate into the essence of all being and significance and to release the fragrance of that inner attainment for the guidance and benefit of others—by expressing in the world of forms, truth, love, purity and beauty—this is the sole game which has intrinsic and absolute worth. All other happenings, incident and attainments in themselves can have no lasting importance. —Meher Baba

We are reborn
in each breath